The Haunting Sliver of Light

a memoir

Karen Rowland

The Haunting Sliver of Light

Copyright © 2022 by Karen Rowland

All rights reserved

ISBN: 979-8-9858764-0-6

Book Designer: Sarah Katreen Hoggatt
10 9 8 7 6 5 4 3 2 1

This book also available in digital formats.

*This book is dedicated to all the survivors and those who
lost their lives to drug abuse and
domestic violence.*

*I would also like to thank the countless family members and
friends who have supported and encouraged me
through the years.*

The Haunting Sliver of Light

Chapter 1

I REMEMBER STARING AT THE SLIVER of light before me. There, in the silence of the darkness, was the only safe place. Our small two bedroom apartment had become our own private HELL! We sat in the corner trembling as I tightly embraced in one arm, my daughter, April, three years old and in the other arm, my son, Christopher, only one year old. The room was thick with the scent of the wood he used to board up the only window in the room. He wanted it to serve as a constant reminder of my last escape attempt and the power he had over me. I can still hear him grunting as he worked up a sweat closing off our only connection to the outside world. I felt we had just sunk into a deep hole as the darkness consumed me. I recall it as though it was yesterday.

The Haunting Sliver of Light

I lowered April into the backyard, gathered my baby boy and his stuffed diaper bag then went to the window to join her. My heart was pounding within my chest as it registered we were just seconds away from freedom. Then he caught me and suddenly it all came crashing down.

He immediately had a firm grip of my hair and continued with the usual wrap around his hand to tighten it up. All too familiar with what was going to happen next I instantly put Christopher down on the floor. As he desperately flung me around throwing me back into the room, he stretched his other arm out the window for April to grab his hand. She knew to cooperate and he reeled her in. He ordered the children to stay in their room as he dragged me by my masterly wrapped hair down the hall into the living room. At first I used to fill with anxiety, heart pounding as I wondered how bad his 'punishment' would be. This time I recalled each and every one of them as I glanced upon balls of my hair, broken fake fingernails, fragments of broken lamps and statues and all kinds of trinkets he had destroyed during his tantrums. It had become a walk down memory lane as I once again heard him tell me he was going to have to teach me another lesson. "You just don't learn do you? You make me do these things to you, Karen. I don't want to. It's your own fault," he insisted as he pulled me to my feet and struck the first blow across my face with his favored back hand. It didn't take as long as the others though. I almost felt like I won that round. I could only hope he was getting as tired of it as I was. He made it clear there was only one door out and he would surely put a bullet in my back if I even tried.

What awaited me within the light was no longer the man I married. He had become a vicious, uncontrollable monster created by a little white powder which had taken control of his very SOUL! My heart ached for the return of my husband but my mind told me it was not to be. I had lost him to the drug world- the drugs had surely taken control of him. He was paranoid of everything. His addiction chipped away pieces of the man he used to be leaving his secrets and lies, his new reality.

The children and I were no longer of any importance to Chris. Only the control he had over us was of any meaning to him. Day after day he told me no other man would ever want a "used woman" like me, especially with two small children. His insulting and degrading rants were the only verbal interaction we had by then. It seemed as though he tried to out-do himself each time and he actually enjoyed it. His arrogant, evil laughs chilled me to my bones. I could *see* the evil which possessed him. It made him feel more powerful to put me beneath him and I saw the horrible monster he had become. As the weeks rolled by, I fell more and more out of love with Chris, left wondering how he could have chosen the drugs over his family. He was supposed to be our protector, instead he was our captor!

He said he had to quit his truck driving job in order to be home to keep an eye on me because he could no longer trust me. He believed I was sleeping with all his friends and his brother while he was out of town trying to make a living. So in order to pay the bills he started to sell drugs. There were people coming and going, day and night. There was no peace, not a moment alone and he never left the apartment except to pick up more drugs. Even then he would leave his "druggy buddies" in charge of us. Under no circumstances were they to let me out of their sight.

At any given moment, fits of anger and rage would overcome him. I never knew exactly when things would flare up again. If I looked at him wrong, there was potential. The fear was overwhelming! His 357 Magnum never left his side. It was loaded and ready to be used at a moment's notice. At times there were impressions of the barrel in my temples where he had pressed just a little too hard the last time.

The time he accused me of posing in a porno magazine is permanently etched in my brain. He made me sit on his lap on the floor with my back against his chest for hours while pressing the gun into my temple with his other arm firmly around my neck. He had me holding the porno rag staring at the picture he insisted was me while screaming in my ear, "Go ahead and tell me that's not you," as he pressed the barrel in further. I silently prayed his trigger finger didn't slip as he became more enraged. I tried to reason with him pointing out the girl in the picture looked nothing like me. She had black hair, mine was strawberry blonde. She had brown eyes while mine were hazel. She had very long pointy fingernails and mine were bitten down due to all the stress. She had very long legs and must have been at least his height if not 6 feet tall and I wasn't even 5 foot. He wasn't going to let me go until I admitted it was me in the photo but I wasn't about to admit to something I didn't do. He angrily screamed, "It's Hollywood. Of course they're going to change your look!" as if he thought I was insulting his intelligence. After hours of insisting it wasn't me he finally relented and told me to make sure it never happened again, but only because it was time for another fix.

The small laundry room in the backyard was off-limits. Unless he was with me and armed I was not allowed out of the apartment. I can still picture him sitting on top of the washer with his steel nosed friend pointed at me as I folded clothes from the dryer. His attention would dart all over the place while he examined the entire yard and its surroundings. I tried to take my time praying someone would come in the yard, with some small hope I would be able to motion to them how desperately I needed their help. But after his visual inspection was complete he turned his focus to me again and ordered me to pick up the pace.

Even when family or friends would call on the phone, he would come up behind me with his trusty old friend 357 digging its nose into my ribs. Only being allowed to say what he made me rehearse I was unable to alert anyone as to the urgency their help was needed. Everyone knew we were having problems and eventually they all stopped calling. I suppose to give us some space and time to work things out oblivious to the real problems and danger we were in. I was too ashamed to confide the harsh reality of the situation to anyone before it got so dangerous. Then when I wanted to, I needed to, I wasn't able to.

It seemed when he started shooting up he began to do more with every fix. It wasn't long before he was out of control. Every nail-hole or little speck he saw on the walls he said was put there by our neighbor who we shared a common wall with. He believed Jerry had installed tiny cameras in those holes to watch us. This was a guy he partied with on a daily basis and suddenly he didn't trust him anymore either. His paranoia was getting out of control.

One day he marched over to Jerry's to tell him he knew all about his tiny cameras and demanded he remove them immediately. Jerry told him he was crazy, there were no cameras and he needed to lay off the meth for a while, he was getting too paranoid then told him to get out of his house.

Chris wouldn't leave and tried to get an enraged confession out of him with threats. He was shaking with mounting adrenaline ready to explode when Jerry pushed him toward the open door and a brawl ensued. They threw each other around Jerry's living room and bloodied each other pretty good, breaking lots of things in their wake. Finally, Chris told Jerry he was going to kill him as he stumbled to his feet leaving Jerry on the floor. He said he was going to shoot him right between the eyes as he held up his fingers in a gun manner and walked out. As far as I knew, they never spoke to each other again. I wasn't allowed to have any contact with Jerry or his wife anymore.

It sure was a strange coincidence when Chris told me only a couple weeks later Jerry was found dead, shot between the eyes! I could feel my own eyes practically pop out of my head when he told me. Goose bumps immediately shot from my head to my toes and I shivered with an instant chill that made my nipples stand at attention. I held my breath and my stare for what felt like an eternity, fearfully waiting for him to tell me if he did it! Then he finally said it was a drug deal gone wrong insinuating *he* had nothing to do with it while leaving it open to my own interpretation, never actually saying if he was involved at all. I desperately wanted to believe him but I had to wonder if it was just another one of his lies.

The Haunting Sliver of Light

Believing I was trying to poison him, he would no longer eat any of the meals I prepared for the children and myself, on the rare occasion he did eat. By then he had lost so much weight and muscle tone he looked like a skeletal image of the handsome, strong young man I married. With his paranoia growing, he was on a constant rampage and wouldn't leave me alone for a second unless I was in the children's room.

Then one day he decided to test our daughter April. He believed in his own warped mind I was indeed hiding drugs from him somewhere in our apartment. He was bound and determined to find them and punish me for it. He figured if anyone besides me knew where the drugs were hidden it would be the children. They were with me every minute of every day. So he asked April if she knew where mommy hid the drugs. Thrilled her daddy was finally showing her some attention she assumed he wanted to play. With an overactive imagination she began to take him on an adventure I will never forget. Because April pointed at the ceiling in the kitchen when he asked her the question he removed all the ceiling panels. Since he found nothing he asked her what was next. She skipped off into the living room and hopped on the couch bouncing a few times. Following behind them in amazement, I watched Chris bounce off the couch exactly like she did and ask her once again, "what next?" April giggled as she watched her daddy copy her every move running into the master bedroom and pointed at the shelf in the closet. He immediately threw me a piercing stare with a look on his face which said he was sure he was going to find something. He went through every box and bag on the shelf and once again found nothing except his own stash. Going from room to room as though it were some kind of treasure hunt or combination to a lock they soon ended up in the children's room. "No April! Don't take him into our "safe place," I desperately cried out. I didn't want his evilness to desecrate our sanctuary but he was sure my reaction was for another reason entirely. He shoved me aside, glared at me with those ice cold eyes and said, "I finally found where you're hiding the goods! Haven't I, bitch?" He rubbed his rough, thinned out hands together and mumbled, "I can't wait to teach her *this* lesson," then added his famous sinister chuckle.

He then decided the reason the children and I spent so much time in their room was because it was where I guarded my hidden treasure. I heard him talking under his breath, he was so mad at himself for not thinking of it sooner. "Of course, she's always in here with the kids. It's got to be in here," he finished mumbling. Then he moved all the furniture away from the walls and looked through all the dresser drawers throwing the children's clothes about the room but again found nothing. He turned to his little tour guide and asked what he needed to do next. April looked around the room for a minute and spotted some crayons on the floor. She picked one up and went around her large dresser with the mirror on it looking up at him for approval. Once he gave her his nodded permission to proceed she started to scribble on the back of it. He desperately followed her lead grabbing a crayon and began to scribble with her, as if this act would unlock a secret door.

It was then there was no doubt in my mind Chris needed professional help. It was beyond me helping him kick a habit. I finally saw he wasn't in the same reality we were. A three-year-old child was making a complete fool out of him and he believed her every step of the way, anxiously hanging on to her every movement. I was scared and anxious of what he might do while also feeling confused about what I should do. It saddened me my husband had done this to us, to himself. As I looked upon his face I realized I didn't know who he was anymore. He portrayed a stranger to me yet wanted me to believe he was still my loving husband who only wanted the best for me and our children.

He was full of excitement as he pulled the back panel off the dresser hoping he had just found his pot of gold at the end of the rainbow. His face went from an ear to ear smile to astounded mouth dropped open and furious he found nothing in his investigation. Within minutes I once again found myself bouncing off walls as he threw me down the hallway and taking blows to my petite 4' 10" frame which could have killed me. He threw me around like a rag doll and anything he could get his hands on went flying across the living room at me. It was impossible for me to stop him or even try to subdue him. All I could do was to endure it until he was exhausted and couldn't think of anymore obscenities to yell at me or anything else to blame me for.

Towering over me at 5′ 11″ tall with the strength of a bulldozer, he just stood there, dripping wet with sweat trying to catch his breath. He stared at me on the floor in the fetal position, bleeding. I could hear the children screaming and crying for me but I learned never to assume he was done and try to get up just because there was a pause in his rage. Sometimes he just had to catch his breath. I didn't dare move until he walked away. It was terrifying and humiliating! I felt like a beaten, scolded dog at his feet. I just prayed he was too tired to continue. When he was done he would always head for the needle to cook up another fix because he had just worked off his high. I hated this had become just another day of our lives.

I WENT BACK THIS TIME ON a mission to save him, our marriage and our family. I loved him and I needed to believe I did everything I possibly could before giving up and moving on. I was so naïve to drugs and what they were doing to him. I really thought I could do it but it was so much bigger than I could have even imagined.

He looked so happy when he answered the door and we were standing there with open arms. He came in for the "hug" then scooted us in. I tried not to show it but I was shaking with fear inside. My heart was pulsating so rapidly I could feel it pushing up on my skin from within my chest as I cautiously walked over the threshold clutching the children. I could feel their little bodies trembling next to mine. I'm sure they felt my fear and it made them scared. Or was it because they remembered what we had left just a few short weeks before?

All at once sad thoughts rushed through my mind and I had to ask myself, "Am I loving him to a point of faulting my children?" I was suddenly nauseated and felt in my gut it was the wrong decision but before I could turn around and verbalize it, he slammed the door shut. It echoed through me like the solid steel door of a dungeon. I looked in his eyes as he glared at me with his usual arrogance. I could see he was quite pleased with himself, convincing me yet again to come back to him. I knew then he wasn't serious about anything he promised me and he wasn't going to let me leave again, not alive. A feeling of panic came over me but I wouldn't let him see it. Damn it! I couldn't give him the satisfaction. It would only strengthen his power and control. I tried desperately to compose myself and show him the little bit of strength I could muster but I knew I was in for trouble.

I quickly made the children's room our refuge. It was the only room in that God-forsaken apartment I convinced him to forbid his entourage to go in. It was an unspoken understanding I didn't even want *him* in there. I never went back to sleeping in "our" bed. He made our bedroom his "office" where all the drug deals, drinking, sex and shooting up until the sun came up took place. The only time I was allowed in our bedroom was when he was forcing me to have sex with him in between the nasty drug whores he screwed. When they weren't around and he wanted some, I was his flavor of the day. I would fight him afraid of what I might catch but it only hurt more when I resisted. It made me sick and it made me despise him even more.

I had lost all hope for a reconciliation and was so tired of being let down by him time after time. I saw the darkness had become my only friend. At least there were a few moments of peace as I stared at the sliver of light from within the darkness. I took several deep breaths to calm my body and get rid of the trembles. I wondered if the children and I would ever get out and have a normal life. Night after night I would pray the children were too young to ever remember the horror and the torture which existed within the light. I hoped and prayed someday soon there would be another chance, a minute or a second he wasn't watching, for another attempt to escape from the nightmare.

The Haunting Sliver of Light

Soon the rising sun would light up the room. The haunting sliver of light would vanish into the morning sunlight. Our quiet, dark, "safe place" would then be like any other room in the apartment. Lit up and left open for the horror and the torture to begin again. "Get some rest," I told myself. For I knew the morning would only bring another challenge for me to face.

Chapter 2

I WENT TO BED PRAYING TO God for the strength and the opportunity for one more escape attempt so I can make it work but I couldn't sleep and wondered why I let him talk me into going back the third time. I should have just stayed away the last time I left but I was desperate to keep my family together and Chris knew exactly how to pull on my heart strings. He talked a big story and made me so many promises. I hopelessly wanted to believe his every word and felt I had to give it one more try. However the third time I finally began to see how it just got worse each time I went back. He was deeper into the drug world not interested in getting out of it. I asked myself, "Why again? Realizing this one more try could get us killed!" I started to reminisce, desperately trying to remember happier times. My mind was searching for memories of Chris and I smiling, laughing and holding each other lovingly when my thoughts took me way back to when we first met.

I think I knew in my heart, almost from the beginning, Chris and I were not meant to be. Maybe I just couldn't admit it to myself. My parents never said it, but I knew they were less than thrilled with my choice for a husband. When I met Chris I was on the rebound from an ever humiliating, "dumped two weeks before the wedding" experience. There were a couple of guys I dated after the wedding was called off, prior to meeting Chris, but nothing serious developed. I was beginning to wonder if something was wrong with me.

Several months had gone by when my friend Nancy lost her father. My family and I went to the viewing to pay our last respects. We were walking up to the door of the funeral home when I noticed 2 young guys about my age checking me out through the large glass door. They each opened one side of the double door as I and my entourage strutted on through. Their eyes were fixed on me as they waited anxiously to see which room my family and I were headed for. I peeked in a couple of viewing rooms then spotted Nancy's mother and made a turn to enter the room as my family followed. We walked up to her to give our condolences hugging her one by one then made our way up to the casket to pay our respects and say a prayer. After, we headed to take a seat when Nancy's mother took hold of my arm and stopped me. She was curious and wanted all the sorted details about my cancelled wedding. I really didn't want to talk about it. I thought I had finally started to get over it and put it behind me. She asked me why Dave called off the wedding when Nancy saved me. "Thank God," I thought. She curled her arm around mine and led me across the room to introduce me to her brother Kelly and his friend Chris. What do you know? They were the 2 guys who were at the front door. After exchanging the polite, it's nice to meet you, we chatted briefly. I learned Kelly had just returned home a few weeks earlier from the Army and Chris was recently home from the Navy. Nancy and her family lived across the street from us and Chris and his older brother Chuck lived with their grandparents around the corner on the next block over. It was a short chat as I don't think they knew what to talk about with a young lady and I was too preoccupied with my own thoughts. I had decided the reason didn't matter so I could move on but Nancy's mother had taken me back to wondering why Dave *did* call off the wedding. He never gave me a reason. I looked around the room as my mind shifted back to Nancy's father. I realized he passed away only two weeks before *her* wedding. Suddenly I couldn't be there any longer. I needed to be home where I could fall on my pillow and cry some more. I found my parents and asked them if we could leave.

The Haunting Sliver of Light

The next morning I woke to my mother standing over me holding a vase with a dozen long stemmed red roses. She said they had just arrived and was very curious who they were from, handing me the mini card to open. It read, "To a beautiful lady. Have a nice day, Chris." I sat there for a moment as my brain took inventory and came up empty handed. Chris? I couldn't think of one guy named Chris I had ever known. Who was this mysterious guy named Chris? I didn't remember Kelly's friend from the day before. Apparently he made little to no impression on me or maybe I was just too saddened by the affairs of the evening to remember him. After all, it was just a brief hello. I got out of bed and called Nancy to see if she could help jog my memory. After hearing about the roses, she chuckled and said, "I didn't think he would actually do it!" "Who?" I asked. "Kelly's friend Chris, remember? After you left last night he told me he thought you were beautiful and wanted to ask you out but he said he was too afraid you would say no. He said you were out of his league then considered if he sent you roses you might feel obligated to go on at least one date with him. I gave him your address but I never thought he would follow through." she explained.

I was flattered so I thought I better get his phone number from her so I could call and thank him for the beautiful roses. Nancy told me to call her back to let her know what happened and we hung up. I called Chris right away. When I thanked him he responded with, "I guess you owe me a date, huh?" then chuckled. I quickly assured him the roses were not necessary, all he had to do was ask. After a brief but pleasant conversation we decided he would pick me up Friday night at 6 p.m.

Before I knew it, it was date night and I hurried home after work. I had just finished touching up my hair and makeup when the doorbell rang. I yelled out, "I'll get it" and ran to the door coming to a screeching halt to take a deep breath before I opened it. It was summer in Las Vegas so I was very surprised to see Chris in a long sleeve shirt when I opened the door. Apparently he read the confused look on my face and began to explain he didn't want my parents to make a rash judgment about him when they saw his tattoos. We chuckled about it for a moment then I grabbed my purse and we were on our way.

He opened the passenger door for me as I asked where we were going. He responded with, "I'm not telling you, it's a surprise." He went around the car, got in and patted the seat while he said, "Move a little closer this big bench seat is so long." He apologized for having to borrow his grandpa's car to take me out followed by his plan of saving money to buy his own. I told him there was no need to apologize.

The Haunting Sliver of Light

In a few minutes I noticed we were getting on the freeway. It was 1979 and I knew Las Vegas wasn't very big so I figured we would be at our destination soon. I turned to face him and got comfortable. Being there were no seatbelts in cars at the time, I was able to slide all the way over to sit right next to him. He began our drive by asking, "Why don't you tell me about yourself and what your idea of the ideal man is." Being somewhat of a chatterbox, I began my journey through childhood, born and raised in Chicago, right up to moving to Las Vegas after high school graduation in June 1978.

I noticed it was dark outside and realized we had been driving quite a while. I looked out the front window and much to my surprise I saw the "Welcome to Arizona" sign!?! Again I asked, "Where are we going? Why are we in Arizona?" He replied, "Remember, it's a surprise, I can't tell you. At this point I'm beginning to wonder if this guy is a psycho. We hadn't lived in Las Vegas very long but I had already heard stories about dead people being found out in the desert and I was becoming concerned. You know how your mind always goes to the worst case scenario first? Okay, just stay calm, I told myself, keep him talking. Or just keep talking to him. I mean, when have you ever heard of a guy driving to another state for dinner on the first date? As my mind was racing with the possibilities of my fate, he began to slow down and veered off the road onto the right shoulder. He brought the car to a stop, opened his door and said, "I want to show you something." He came around the car and opened my door as a gentleman would. I hesitantly got out as he gently reached for my hand. It was pitch black but he led me over to the far right edge of the shoulder and the moment he mentioned it was the Virgin River I got chills down my spine. I could hear the water rushing down below but my vision was "ZIP"! I started to back up and felt his arms grab me around my waist from behind. "I won't let you fall in," he said. "Maybe we should come back in the daylight when you can actually see the beautiful scenery." He turned me around to head back to the car. Thank God! We got in and he said, "We don't have too much farther to go."

As we entered the freeway again, I asked about him. I had to find out all I could, it might work to my advantage if the night should get hairy. He told me his story as I listened carefully trying to make a mental note of all the important facts.

He said he was from Bellflower, California. His father had left his mother when she was pregnant with him and his older brother, Chuck wasn't quite a year old. His mother June remarried and had two more boys, Kelly and Steven. As the years rolled on and the boys began to grow into strapping eating machines, June and her husband, Chuck (how ironic he had the same name as her first born) realized they couldn't afford to support all four children anymore. June was in between jobs, this particular stretch being longer than usual and Chuck was considerably older than June. He was collecting a disability check every month while waiting to reach retirement age to add social security to his income. They decided to send Chuck and Chris to Las Vegas to live with their maternal grandparents, Grandma and Grandpa McGaughey. The boys were only 10 and 11 years old when they were sent on a greyhound bus together across the desert. He mentioned he was in the Navy for two years right out of high school but said he was dishonorably discharged for screwing a captain's wife. It seemed he got some pleasure out of bragging about it for a minute then said he had gotten home only two weeks before Nancy's father died. I turned my head again to glance out the window only to see a sign in the short distance. "Welcome to Utah"!!!!! "Okay, I really need to know where you're taking me! We have gone through two states and I'm not feeling very comfortable anymore! Utah??" I exclaimed. Chris just giggled and said, "We're just about there. I promise, I'm not a psycho." I couldn't believe he said it! What is he, psychic?"

About 10 minutes later we entered the small town of St. George, Utah. He drove up a long, winding road to the top of a hill and pulled into the parking lot of Jeremiah's Steakhouse. He had made reservations for two and even had roses and a bottle of wine chilling on the table. I don't know how he got away with the wine since we were only 18 years old but what a romantic touch I thought.

Right then, I didn't feel 18 at all. We were on a romantic date in a restaurant with a bottle of wine on the table. Up until then, I was never allowed to indulge in a glass of wine. Not that I wanted to. I was still in the frame of mind that only adults could drink alcohol and I wasn't 21 yet. It was like a stepping stone into adulthood. I don't believe I ever had a taste of alcohol before that evening but I did have a glass of wine with my meal. We had a wonderful dinner and conversation. He was respectful, charming, and funny, I was actually starting to like him. I'm not sure if it was because I felt bad for his childhood or it was just him. Either way, I was surprised. He asked if I would mind if we stopped off at a friend's house when we got back to Vegas. By the end of the evening I was feeling pretty comfortable with him and said, "of course not." He said he had to show me off because his friends would never believe him. We laughed about it as we got back in the car to head home.

When we got to his friend's house and went in we found about five guys sitting in the living room passing around a joint. He introduced me to them as I struggled to catch my breath standing in a big cloud of smoke. I was only around marijuana once before in high school. I was peer pressured into trying a puff and didn't like how it made me feel. I wasn't in control and I never did it again. Suddenly I wasn't feeling too comfortable there. The room was filled with smoke and I was choking on it waving my hand through the air to clear the smoke from my face. I guess Chris could sense I wanted to go so he told his friends he would catch up with them later and we left. In hindsight, I believe that's when I began to settle, without even realizing it. Up until then, I wouldn't have anything to do with someone who did any kind of drugs, even marijuana. It was my first red flag to turn the other way but I settled. In that moment I subconsciously adjusted my criteria, my standards by which I chose those to be around, to accept the marijuana use because I liked him and I was on the rebound needing to feel wanted and loved again.

We drove back to my house and sat in the car for a while chatting. Then I saw my mom peek out the living room window which was usually my cue to call it a night and get in the house. I fiddled with my purse a little, nervously waiting for him to lean in to kiss me goodnight but he didn't. So I thanked him for a lovely evening and got out of the car. I could feel his intense stare practically burning a hole in my back as he outlined my every move up to the door. I was hoping he was going to be romantic and come running up the driveway to stop me just as I was going to step through the door, but no. He didn't even *try* to kiss me.

SEVERAL MONTHS AFTER HER HUSBAND'S FUNERAL, Nancy's mother moved to Utah leaving Nancy and her new husband Joe to look after the house.

Her brother Kelly also lived with them and we all hung out together at their house. Chris could see his friend Kelly was also smitten with me. Kelly would kiss me and cling to me every time Chris was around as if he was marking his territory and we could all tell Chris didn't like it at all. But because Chris never asked me out again I didn't put a label on us as a couple. In fact he didn't even act as though he wanted to be a couple all the times we hung out together. I felt as though we were just friends or I wouldn't have even kissed Kelly back. I actually liked both of them. I think he finally decided he better declare us exclusive before he lost me to his friend and he did. We started seeing each other and were soon inseparable. Notice I didn't say dating? I can't remember any other dates Chris took me on other than our first one. He was my date for a Christmas party at the bank I worked at but we never went on another actual date.

After only a few months Chris proposed. I was very surprised and asked him why so soon? He told me he found himself daydreaming about me and our life together while he was stopped at a red light. He was so caught up in his fantasy he didn't notice the light had turned green until everyone behind him started beeping their horns at him. He giggled a little and said it was a sign to him. He said he never met anyone who made him dream of a future together. He knew I was the one. He was positive we were meant to be. He made it sound so romantic I fell for him hook, line and sinker.

When I accepted his proposal he couldn't contain his excitement. He grabbed me around the waist, lifted me off the ground and spun us around. He was on cloud nine and I was right there with him.

A couple of days later he called me as giddy as a school girl. I asked him what he was so happy about and he said, "You agreed to be my wife and now I have something for you. I have to see you tonight." I told him I was doing the dinner dishes and to give me about 15 minutes before he came over and we hung up. I was suddenly so excited. I went outside when he rang the doorbell so we could have some privacy. He greeted me with a very long, romantic kiss then got down on one knee to put my new engagement ring on my finger and made it official. We went inside to tell my family but I could tell they were not thrilled with the news. I wasn't going to let them ruin our happy mood so Chris and I left.

We went straight to Nancy and Joe's to start spreading the news. Then we headed for Grandpa and Grandma McGaughey. They already knew he was going to propose and were so excited to hear I accepted. Chris wanted to tell everyone so we made the rounds in the neighborhood and tried to find as many of his friends as possible. We ended up at Jamey and Sue's house. It was the first time I met them. They were both friends of his who were high school sweethearts and were newly married. Jamey worked in construction and Sue was going to college to be a teacher, pregnant with their first child. Chris told me they were the only ones of all his friends who had it together already, beginning adulthood, where everyone else was still in party mode. He wanted me to get close to Sue since we were getting married. He said she was a good woman, like me, not at all like the party type girls who hung out at the bars getting drunk every night with the guys.

Sue and I immediately took a liking to each other. We were both short and feisty. She appeared to be about 6 months pregnant and confirmed it when I asked her. The guys were catching up in the living room while Sue and I got to know each other in the kitchen. We were drawn to each other and connected on a personal level right away. We felt like we could confide things to one another almost instantly and had a very pleasant conversation. Finally, I thought, someone on my wave length. I noticed it was getting late so I motioned to Chris with a nod of my head in the direction of the door. I told them it was a pleasure to meet them and I knew we were going to be good friends. Sue said she felt the same and told me to call if there was anything she could do to help with the preparations for the wedding.

It was just before the holidays and Chris wanted to get married as soon as possible suggesting a Christmas wedding but I wanted to take our time planning our perfect wedding and didn't want to have to rush it or have it clouded by the holidays. He didn't want to wait but agreed to a beautiful summer wedding. We began our planning but in December I was having suspicions I might be pregnant. I was very nauseous and tired all the time so I went to the store and bought a home pregnancy test. Sitting on the toilet, steadily holding the wand in the stream of my urine, I was already sure I was pregnant. I never felt sick in that way before and certainly not every day. But how was it possible? I always thought I couldn't have children. At least it's what I remember the gynecologist say when I was diagnosed with endometriosis at the age of 13. I always prayed the doctor was wrong. I wanted children someday. I never used birth control because of her telling us I would probably never be able to have children. I gasped and thanked God I had still used the good old school Catholic rhythm method of birth control just in case. Believe it or not, the nuns taught it to us in biology in high school when we learned about our menstrual cycle and how babies were made.

I began to fill with excitement as I cleaned up. This was a miracle if it were true! I washed my hands and grabbed the wand trying to conceal it as I fast walked back to my bedroom. While anxiously waiting for the results I paced the floor. If I was pregnant, I wondered how Chris would feel about starting our life together with a baby right away. I thought, "How could he be anything but happy though? I know it would be a little harder for us but we would manage." Finally it was confirmed by a little plus sign. I was pregnant. My mom walked in as I threw the wand in the trash. I turned toward the door as I heard it open and started to cry when our eyes met. She asked me what was wrong. I had already told myself not to tell anyone just yet if it was positive but I felt compelled to tell her the truth right then. Although she would rather I waited until we were married to have a baby, she was so happy she was going to be a grandma. She hugged me and told me to get in to the doctor as soon as possible. I told her I would and asked her to please not tell my dad yet and she agreed.

I wanted to tell Chris first so I called him and asked him to come over. He could tell something had me worried and was there immediately. I told him he was going to be a father and he beamed from ear to ear. I was relieved he seemed very happy about my news. I explained to him I didn't want to be eight months pregnant at our wedding nor did I want to wait to get married after we had the baby. I wanted to be married when our baby arrived. He agreed and was happy we were getting married sooner like he originally wanted to. We changed the wedding date to February 23, 1980 and ordered the invitations. We were so happy. Chris decided to go out apartment hunting with his brother, Chuck. He said he thought it was a good idea to have Chuck live with us so we could split the bills to make it a little easier since none of us had ever lived on our own yet and we all agreed. I was just happy to be getting married and have my own place, it didn't matter to me. I was on cloud nine. My dreams of getting married and having my own family were finally coming true. I could hardly believe it. Although in the back of my mind I was terrified Chris might get a case of cold feet just like Dave did. I didn't know if I would be able to handle it again especially being pregnant this time. I tried to put it to rest and told myself not to worry about it, just get caught up in all the wedding plans and be happy.

Chris asked me what my dream house looked like. I told him I liked the white pillars on either side of the front door then chuckled. I didn't think we would have a house like that until we were well into our 30's if not 40's but a girl could dream. Then one day when he picked me up from work he surprised me and took me to see our new apartment. When he pulled up in front of the complex he pointed at the two massive pillars standing at attention as they guarded the front entrance and he said, "There's your white pillars." I was so surprised, my mouth dropped open. He looked pretty proud of himself as he turned into the driveway and continued to the back parking lot. He parked the car, led me to our second floor apartment and was strutting like a proud peacock as he gave me a tour of our first home together.

It was a cute, furnished two story apartment. The living room, dining room, kitchen and half bath were on the first floor. I just loved the curved staircase which led up to two bedrooms with a full bathroom in the middle. Each bedroom had a sink and mirror for shaving too. I loved it but didn't want to get too attached because the complex didn't except children. Chris was so excited he found a complex with my pillars he didn't care if we had to move in 6 months and I didn't have the heart to give him crap about it. We were ecstatic! Before we were married was the happiest part of our entire relationship. He cared about what I wanted, what I thought, he wanted to please me and he always wanted to be with me.

Shortly after the invitations were mailed out my girlfriend Patti had a bridal shower for me at her house. She had so much food and a bunch of games to play with prizes for each winner. Patti and I worked together at the bank in a 10 girl office. All the girls were there along with more from other departments, Sue and Nancy, my mom, my 2 grandmothers and Patti's mom too. We had a blast and they were all very generous with the beautiful gifts they gave. After several hours of fun and food I was getting pretty tired and decided to say my goodbyes. I thanked everyone and found mom and my grandmothers as they were finishing their goodbyes. After we got the gifts in my little Pinto hatchback we headed home. On the way, I informed them I was going to drop them off at home then take all the gifts to the apartment. There was no sense in unloading the gifts only to load them again to take them to the apartment after we were married in a few more weeks. Mom agreed and they all started sharing compliments about the gifts everyone gave. Once the ladies were safe and sound in the house I took off.

I drove up to the apartment complex and smiled when I saw the pillars. I wondered if my soon to be husband did the same. I went up and found the guys hanging out drinking beer, smoking pot and watching television. Another ignored red flag. We were only 19 and they were always drinking and smoking. I didn't drink alcohol but I accepted their choice of underage drinking. I told them the car was full of gifts from the shower and they enthusiastically jumped up and headed for the door to carry them up. We checked out each gift with excitement, wrapped them back up and put the collection on the kitchen table to put away later. I was so exhausted I went upstairs to the bedroom to lie down and fell sound asleep. Chris didn't want to wake me so he just crawled in bed next to me and went to sleep.

I woke in a panic the next morning around 9am. I jumped out of the bed and yelled to him as he rubbed his eyes, "Oh my God! I have to go! My dad is going to be pissed!" He said, "Your dad? You're 19 and engaged. Who cares what your dad thinks?" "*I* care what my dad thinks!" I shouted at him as I ran down the stairs to grab my purse and head out the door. Just then the phone rang and made me jump out of my skin. I answered since I was closest to the phone and sure enough, it was my dad. Boy was he mad! He demanded I get home immediately. Really, I thought, I'm 19 for goodness sake AND engaged. I heard Chris say it as it ran through my head. But my dad was old fashioned and didn't believe I should be spending the night with a guy unless we were married.

I rushed home only to be greeted by the whole family. My mom was the only one in my family who knew I was pregnant and she wasn't supposed to tell anyone but when they woke up and saw I wasn't home, she panicked. Thinking something happened to me, she blurted out, "And she's pregnant!" I honestly think my dad was more upset about the fact I was pregnant before getting married than him not knowing anything about it. He was furious and yelled, "Pack your things and go shack up with him like you have been," he spit out. I knew then mom had spilled the beans. I put my head down like a scolded child and started to my room. My dad was right behind me as he continued to yell about how disappointed he was in me. His mother was right behind him pointing at me while yelling "You're going to make him have a heart attack!" He had just had a triple bypass the year before and we were all still a little worried about his health. Dad reached to the shelf in my closet, got down a suitcase for me and threw it on my bed. "Get your shit packed and get out of my house," he demanded again as he turned to leave the room waving his hand for everyone else to get out also.

I packed some things while the tears poured down my face. I was scared my dad wouldn't want to walk me down the aisle or even come to my wedding. I truly felt his disappointment and it hurt. I fell on my bed and began to sob. Soon my mom walked in. She told me she talked to him and when he calmed down he realized he reacted in haste and out of anger. He decided he didn't want me to leave after all. She said she told him it was a time when we all needed to come together. I went to talk to him and told him how sorry I was I had disappointed him but all I could do was to move forward and try to make better choices. He seemed to forgive me even though he was not pleased with my actions or my choice for a husband. It was unspoken however. I knew he didn't think Chris was good enough for me. In all fairness, I believe Chris was right. He was basing his opinion on Chris' appearance because of his tattoos. He hadn't taken the time to get to know him yet. I just knew things would get better after we were married and they had a chance to bond. A girl could hope, right?

THE HOLIDAYS WERE OVER AND THE wedding plans were in full swing with only a month to go. We had most of the R.S.V.P.'s back, the guys were all just about measured for their tux's and mom and dad offered to pay for all the food for the reception and have it at their house. I decided to wear the wedding dress I had kept from my pending marriage to Dave. Some people told me it was bad luck and I shouldn't do it but I loved the dress and couldn't afford to buy another one.

Finally my wedding day was almost here. After rehearsal the night before, all my bridesmaids spent the night at my house so we could all get ready for the wedding together. My father's friend Dave was an aspiring photographer and offered to take all the pictures as a wedding gift. He got to the house early so he could get pictures of all the preparations and decorations then we all headed to the church. Dave must have taken over a hundred pictures before the wedding. We were outside with the sun blaring and were all getting a bit hot when someone said it was time to go in for the nuptials. It was a short ceremony at a nondenominational church because I was baptized and raised Catholic but Chris was baptized Mormon so neither church would marry us without the other converting.

The guys were all so handsome in their tuxedos. Chris wore a white tuxedo to match my dress while all his groomsmen wore black tuxedos. My bridesmaids looked beautiful in their sky blue dresses with matching big floppy hats. They all lived in Las Vegas except my best friend from high school, Juliana. She had an emergency appendectomy just a week before and still came out for the wedding. I felt so bad for her. She was obviously still in pain, walking a little hunched over, holding her stomach. She walked slowly too but it didn't matter to me, she was there. It was the first time Chris and my new friends met her. I didn't see it at the time but Chris took a liking to her. It would be many, many years before I would find out my soon to be husband propositioned my best friend, Juliana, my maid of honor, the day before our wedding.

Chapter 3

WE HAD A BEAUTIFUL WEDDING AND a wonderful reception at my parents' house then left for our first night in our apartment as husband and wife. The next day, Juliana caught her flight home and we took off for California to go to Disneyland for our honeymoon.

Chris' parents still lived in Bellflower and offered for us to stay with them to save money. We only had a little cash to work with so we thanked them and took them up on their offer. Every night we were there Chris was out partying with his brothers, dad and old friends while I was left in the apartment with his mother, June. I loved her but it was our honeymoon! As soon as we were married the way my husband treated me changed. He said he was just celebrating and I needed to lighten up but I wanted him to celebrate with me. It was *our* wedding but he wanted to party with the boys so

The Haunting Sliver of Light

I was left with my new mother-in-law. I thought, maybe I should just lighten up and let him party with the guys. I was pregnant and couldn't drink anyway, I rationalized. I had already begun to justify his bad choices without even realizing it. I was just trying to make good of an awkward situation. On the bright side, it did give June and I some girl time to get better acquainted. We had some great talks and grew close pretty quick. By the end of our 3 day trip we felt like we had known each other for years. When she hugged Chris goodbye I heard her whisper in his ear, "If you're not good to her, she is going to leave you." She didn't like how he went off with his friends every day and after 3 days of heart to heart talks she realized I wasn't the type of woman who was going to put up with that kind of treatment for too long. She could see how embarrassed and upset I was every time my new husband told me he was taking off with the boys and how he shot me down each time I tried to talk to him in private. I think June knew from the get go Chris and I would not last and she was trying to warn him.

From the beginning, my husband was not coming home after work. He would stay out until the wee hours of the morning, sometimes getting home in just enough time to take a shower and leave for work. All through my pregnancy, Chris and Chuck would have parties at the apartment or go out partying. I would always leave a light on and go to bed. I remember lying in the dark, staring at the crack of light in the hallway, wondering where he was and what he was doing. I knew he was with other women but my heart couldn't bear the thought. He made me feel like I was no longer worth his time and every night he wasn't home with me, chiseled away at my self-esteem and self-worth. Little by little, I lost pieces of me. I was so lonely and began to think he was turned off by my growing body and he just didn't think I was attractive anymore. I wasn't good enough for him to be faithful. He seemed to be very uninterested in spending any time at all with me and was only interested in telling me what I could and couldn't do while he was out doing whatever he wanted.

My friend Patti and her husband Joe moved into our complex shortly after we did and lived just down the hall from us. They saw all too soon how often Chris wasn't home. I think Patti felt bad for me because she used to tell Joe to grab my trash on his way down to the dumpster. I was really trying not to smoke while I was pregnant but truth be known, Chris had me so stressed out most of the time, sometimes I would run down to Patti's apartment just to take a few puffs. He even "caught" me smoking one time at work when he unexpectedly dropped in and scolded me like a child right in front of all my coworkers. It was so embarrassing. I spent some of my evenings after work with Patti and Joe before turning in for the night, as not to be home alone. It sure beat sitting in the silent loneliness my new home had come to be.

CHUCK AND I HAD A GOOD friendship and had a few heart-to-heart talks by then. He said he told Chris he was crazy for being out partying when he had a good wife at home with a baby on the way. In fact, he told me most of their old neighborhood friends also told him the same thing. There were times when Chuck would come home to shower and change before going out after work but not Chris. I began to think it was because he wanted to save himself, and me I guess, the trouble of an argument about him going out when it didn't matter anyway. He was still going to leave to go out and play no matter what I said; it wasn't going to change his mind.

Sometimes Chuck would have dinner with me so I didn't have to eat alone again and then there were times Chuck would come home late without Chris because they got separated between bars. I would hear him come in and go to bed. I'd be waiting to hear Chris come in next but he never did. I couldn't sleep and would just lay there waiting for my husband, silently crying. Sometimes I would cry for hours while I was talking to God and asking Him why? Begging Him to let my husband walk in the door and tell me he loved me and he realizes the baby and I mean the world to him. Please let him tell me he is done with the partying and ready to be a husband and father. Much to my heartache, such a day was nowhere in sight.

I remember one time I woke Chuck up to go look for Chris. It was well over an hour he had been home and I was so worried and in panic mode thinking Chris was lying in a gutter somewhere, hurt. I felt guilty afterwards because Chuck was drunk and passed out. He shouldn't have even been driving but I was desperate. Chris was starting to pull away from me and his childhood friends. He was making connections with new friends where he was introduced down another path with new bars to hang out at. These bars had more than just pool tables and liquor. They held a dark, alluring entertainment of strippers and the biker scene which my husband had taking a liking to. I believed he loved it more than he loved me.

THERE WAS A LARGE PORTRAIT OF me at 18 years old in the dining area, which I loved. I never really liked pictures of myself but it was a good one and it was a gift from a photographer boyfriend I dated just before my husband. Chris said he loved the picture and insisted on hanging it up in the apartment.

One very restless night, late in my pregnancy, I went downstairs to get a glass of ice water. While I was sitting at the kitchen table, Chris and his friend, Jeff, came in the door. They were both falling down drunk and I suspected high on something. He immediately accused me of waiting up for him just to bitch at him for staying out late and flew into a drunken rage. As he barreled toward me, I stood up and put my left arm up in front of my face to protect myself as I saw him raise his hand to me. He grabbed the glass out of my other hand and threw it right at my picture. I could not believe my eyes! He grabbed my arms and squeezed as he screamed at me. The picture crashed to the floor and pieces of glass, the wood frame, ice and water went flying all over the small dining area. Horrified, I stood there trembling and crying as he continued to yell at me and belittle me in front of his friend. Suddenly he released my arms pushing me away from him. I stumbled backwards and caught myself grabbing a chair just before I was going to fall to the floor. This was the first time things were of a violent and physical nature. I remember thinking I didn't know who he was anymore. It was supposed to be one of the happiest times of our marriage, waiting for our first child to be born but he made my pregnancy months so lonely and stressful, I couldn't even enjoy it. I took off up the stairs pausing in the middle. I was so hurt and upset I mustered up the courage to give him something to think about. Turning around to interrupt his drunken rambling, I yelled out, "You think you're fit to be a father? FUCK YOU!" and stomped up to our bedroom.

I heard the front door slam as I collapsed on our bed balling. I waited a short while to see if he was going to come back but he didn't. I got up to wipe the tears streaming down my face and blow my nose. Then I went downstairs to clean up the mess I was sure he left behind. Much to my surprise, my picture was gone. I checked the trash but it wasn't in there either. He must have taken it with him. I cleaned up the best I could and went back up to bed to try to get some sleep before he came home to blame me some more.

I lay in bed trying to breathe through my stuffy nose with my head pounding from crying so hard. I was almost out when I heard Chris come in the door. My eyes darted to the bedside table to check the time. It was a couple of hours later. He came straight up to the bedroom with my picture in his hands, showed it to me and apologized for ruining it. It was cut up beyond repair. He got in bed and lay down next to me. He told me he sat in the parking lot staring at my picture the entire 2 hours, thinking and crying. Then he nestled up against me wrapping his arms around me and rested one of his rough, manly hands on my enormous baby bump. I could feel his love at that very moment and it filled my heart with hope. I felt so content in his arms and remember thinking, this is how it's supposed to be. Will my prayers finally be answered? Did he finally realize he is destroying our marriage and needs to stop his selfish behavior? Please God, let it be so. Then he dropped a bomb on me and told me he thought I should leave him and move back in with my parents! He said he was sorry, again, and told me I deserved better than him. But we were expecting our first child! I asked him if it was what he wanted because I wanted to stay and work things out. He said no. We held each other tight and wept. I said, "I don't understand. If you know how you're treating me is wrong, why do you continue to do it?" He couldn't give me an explanation and of course he promised again it wouldn't happen anymore. I desperately wanted to believe him.

Just a couple days later he came home from work late, about 10 p.m. It was obvious to me he was high on something and when I confronted him, he showed me a little piece of paper with a picture of Mickey Mouse on it. He said it was a hit of acid and he ate a couple of hits just a while ago. It sounded crazy to me. I never heard of such a thing before. "You ate paper with drugs in it?" I asked to clarify. He shook his head affirmatively. "OK, so what does it do to you?" I continued. He started giggling and said, "It makes you hallucinate." Great! I silently prayed I would be sound asleep before his Alice in Wonderland story began. He seemed to be himself so I told him I was going to bed and he followed me upstairs. After a few more minutes it started to kick in I guess because he started acting goofy and began to tickle me. I tried pushing him away, telling him to stop. Normally I would have soaked up the attention from him as it was rare but I'm not going to lie, I was upset he came home late and high AGAIN!! Really, we just had a major blow up a couple days ago about this very issue and you do it again? I thought. I wanted to discuss it but it was clear he was in no condition to discuss anything more important than Mickey Mouse. I just wanted to go to sleep but he kept it up. He was getting annoying so I went downstairs to sleep on the couch. Shortly after I got comfortable he came downstairs and insisted on pitching a tent in the living room except he believed we were in the middle of the WOODS! He brought several blankets with him which he used to make his flimsy tent. I went along with his charade hoping he would shut up and I could get some sleep but he tormented me for at least another hour. "Oh man, did you hear that?" he asked. He insisted there was a bear outside of our "tent" sniffing around. Being so inexperienced and naïve to drugs, I did not know how to react or what to expect so I just played along with him about the bear. I didn't want to do anything to upset him given I had seen a violent side of him a few days before. I just wanted to sleep. Trying to appease him I just let him ramble on and tell me his story until we both finally fell asleep.

In the morning it was business as usual. He showered, dressed and was ready to leave within 30 minutes. Sometimes it was before I was even awake. In fact, I think he preferred it that way. No discussion, apology or even a word about the night before and the fact he did some kind of drug, yet again. I was getting increasingly concerned about it and wanted to discuss it with him but he was not on the same page. It was becoming more apparent he did not care about what I thought or felt anymore and he was going to do exactly what he wanted to regardless of what I said so there was no need to even discuss it. I was getting so tired of pleading and begging for any little scrap of his time and attention yet I found myself making excuses to justify his behavior in my own mind. It was easier than to admit our marriage was already falling apart. I told myself in a way it was good he was getting all his partying out of the way, so to speak, before the baby came. This way he would be present and more focused on his family once our little miracle arrived. I ended up justifying his bad choices anyway I could to make myself feel a little better.

Soon we had to move from the "adult only" apartment complex so Chris decided we would move in with his grandparents. We didn't discuss anything about the move, he just told me one day what his plan was. Grandma and Grandpa McGaughey were the sweetest, kindest old couple already in their 80's. We had a really good relationship and they could hardly wait for the birth of their great grandchild. They welcomed me into their home and always treated me like family. I spent a lot of time with them and we got very close as Chris' night time behavior continued. I was on maternity leave from the bank and getting ready for the baby. I would clean the house for Grandma McGaughey and help her with dinner and dishes every night. Then we would retire to the living room for a little television time together with Grandpa McGaughey while he brought us up to speed about the hot topics in the news.

Late one night, after everyone was in bed, Chris came home from drinking all night and jumped in the bathtub. I waited over an hour for him to get out of the tub and come to bed but he never did so I got up to check on him. When I went in the bathroom I found him sound asleep, snoring with his nose only about an inch above the water. It was so muggy in there and reeked of puke. He had thrown up in the tub and there were chunks of food floating around in the murky water. I fought to hold back throwing up myself as I seemed to gag every 5 seconds scooping up the partially digested pieces of his favorite bar food, chicken fingers and fries. Added with the stench of beer and hard liquor made it next to impossible to keep my own dinner in my stomach were it belonged. Once I had removed the big chunks I woke him up, drained the tub and washed him as he struggled to stay standing in the shower. I had to get the puke smell off of him or I would be gagging all night. I tucked him in, cleaned the tub with bleach then went back to bed. He was so out of it he was passed out again oblivious to the fact we were finally laying in the same bed together. I was so upset with him yet I felt a sense of contentment knowing my husband was finally home with me. I laid there considering if it was a mistake marrying him and couldn't help but wonder if it was a sign of what the rest of our marriage would be like. I remembered him saying I deserved better and he was right. I couldn't understand why his hurtful behavior continued.

Some nights, the guys and their friends would be hanging out, drinking in front of the house with the garage door open. Our bedroom was right next to the garage so I couldn't fall asleep hearing all the noise from their front yard party but at least he was home. I'd lie in bed yearning for just a tiny piece of his time and attention he gave to his friends every night yet there I was again in the dark staring at the sliver of light from the window waiting for my husband to come to bed with me. I was so desperate to feel his love again, I would even stand on the bed and peek out the window just to get a glimpse of him to satisfy my deep longing for his touch. Everything else seemed to always be more important to Chris than me and our unborn child developing inside of me which he showed no interest in either. I always wondered why he asked me to marry him. If all he wanted to do was party, why get married at all?

Chapter 4

PATTI HAD A BABY SHOWER FOR me just before we moved in with Chris' grandparents and all the gifts were set aside to go through later so I decided to wash all the baby clothes and set up the tiny area in our room we designated for our new addition. I was hanging the adorable little sleepers and onesies on the clothes line in the back yard when I felt what I thought was a contraction. Yep, by the time I was finished hanging the clothes I had felt another. They were far apart throughout the day but things got more intense during the night so early the next morning we headed to the hospital. On September 17, 1980, at 11:10 p.m. after 22 hours of hard labor, my beautiful baby girl, April Nichole was born. Chris was there for the entire 22 hours, sort of. Of course he was complaining it was taking too long as if I had any control over it. He wanted to leave and come back later but I told him it was out of the question and he had to stay. Instead, he took breaks and went out to the parking lot to have a beer and smoke a joint. However once we were in the delivery room he was a captive audience.

I had been asking for something for the pain for quite a while and was told I had to go through some of the labor first without the epidural. By the time I was brought into the delivery room the baby was crowning. The bed they wheeled me in on was placed right in front of a huge, round mirror up in the corner of the room so I could watch the birth. I could see my baby's head and assumed it wouldn't be much longer when someone finally came in to administer the epidural. While I was busy breathing through a horrendous contraction they were applying alcohol to my back and instructing me to hold still or I could end up paralyzed. I remember yelling, "I don't need it now. It's too late. I don't want it now." But they told me to bring my knees up to my chest and don't move. Really, how do you bring your knees to your chest when you have a huge belly with a baby in it?

Within seconds I could no longer feel anything from the waist down. I was angry. I told them I changed my mind about the epidural. I wanted to experience my baby's birth all natural since it was almost over anyway. It was too late. The doctor came in and ordered me to bear down as the next contraction came. No longer being able to feel the birth of my baby, I focused on what I had left. My eyes were fixed on the enormous mirror as

I watched my first baby come into our world and take her first breath. He cut the umbilical cord and handed her to the nurse to clean up and weigh. Then I couldn't believe my eyes when I looked back and saw him in the mirror. He had his arm up to his elbow inside me! I asked in disbelief, "What are you doing?" "Fishing around for the placenta which never came out" he replied. Then in a few seconds he said, "Oh, here it is" as he pulled it out. He sewed me up and took my baby from the nurse laying my gorgeous tiny baby girl on top of my chest. At that very moment I knew I was blessed with a miracle from God. My eyes weld up with tears as I kissed and kissed her tiny bald head and beautiful soft silky face. She grasped my pinky finger in her wee little hand as I gently raised it to my lips for a kiss. I had never witnessed anything so beautiful and I knew I had never felt so much love in my heart before. My beautiful miracle opened up a part of my heart I never knew existed. Suddenly my heart was over flowing with love and joy as I was overcome with emotion and began to sob with happiness.

As soon as the doctor introduced us to our beautiful little daughter April, Chris said, "We will be back in a year to try again for a boy!" It stunned me and broke my heart at the same time. How dare he? I was so embarrassed but too exhausted to put up a fight. I just wanted to kiss and stare at my beautiful baby all night. I shook my head in disapproval and ignored him shifting my attention back to the miracle God had just given me. She was so perfect I couldn't take my eyes off of her. As I checked her little feet, hands and face I realized the enormous responsibility my new miracle came with.

Just as I was out of the delivery room Chris was ready to leave. He didn't even want to wait for me to get settled into my room for the night. I hoped and prayed he would want to stay the night with April and I. Hell no! It was time to party!!! He had an excuse this time. It wasn't quite midnight so he knew there was a party somewhere in full swing. He wanted to brag to everyone about being a dad. Turned out, he had no idea what being a dad was all about.

THE NEXT MORNING THE NURSE BROUGHT my beautiful baby girl to me to breastfeed for the first time and I almost drowned her. My breasts had grown to a gigantic I cup and were so filled with milk, when April began to suck, it poured out. Milk went up her tiny nose and gushed down her throat and she was turning blue! I screamed for the nurse while I held the baby up. The milk just continued to pour out of my breast soaking me, April and the bed. The nurse took April to clean her up and feed her a bottle in the nursery while another nurse cleaned up the mess and changed the bed. It scared me enough to decide not to try again just yet since

April was perfectly content with the formula they gave her in the nursery. I thought maybe I would try again when we were home and my breasts went down a little.

Both sides of the family came to visit and welcome our new bundle of joy to the family. Grandpa McGaughey said he thought April looked just like him because she was as bald as he was. She did have a little white peach fuzz which I remember thinking with a grin, made her resemble him even more. The next day we were both released and we went to Grandpa and Grandma McGaughey's, April's first home. They doted on her and loved her so much but Chris began to argue a lot with his Grandpa. Grandpa McGaughey tried to tell him his party days had to be over now that he had a family but Chris didn't want to hear it. He would tell him to mind his own business and he was a grown man who could do whatever he wanted. Grandpa McGaughey told him what he wanted didn't matter anymore. It should come after what is best for his family but Chris was too young and selfish to listen. Chris and I were the same age but I think we were in two separate worlds when it came to our maturity.

My breasts were so full, they were always leaking. So I started to pump my breasts thinking I would get rid of all the milk. Haha. Little did I know at the time, the more you pump, the more the milk comes in. Within a couple of weeks I had 5 gallons of mothers' milk in the fridge. It obviously wasn't working so I finally called the doctor and he told me to bind the breasts in the tightest bra I had for about a week. No more pumping and the breasts will not produce any more milk. I followed his instructions and it worked. There was no more milk but my breasts didn't go down in size. I thought of having a breast reduction but decided to wait at least a year to see if losing the baby weight would help them go down some. Besides, when I mentioned it to Chris he might as well have forbid me to do it.

April was only a couple of months old when we housesat for our friends, Joe and Nancy. They were going to Utah to visit family for a few weeks. I loved Grandpa and Grandma McGaughey very much but I hoped the time we would have alone with our new baby would help us grow and bond as a family. I prayed Chris would see how beautiful our little family was and realize the responsibilities we had as parents. Surely he can see this tiny, innocent human being needed us for everything. There was no more time for parties and behaving as though he didn't have a care in the world. She was counting on us to be present, responsible and provide for her. I hoped with all my heart he would make a change for the better but his shenanigans continued. I was happy to be right across the street from my parents where April and I would go almost every night for some company. The only good to come of it was Chris realized he didn't want to live with anyone anymore. He wanted the freedom of being able to do whatever he wanted without having to be scolded for it by his elders. He didn't care what *I* said, he would just tell me to shut up and deal with it.

When Joe and Nancy returned from their trip we rented a house around the corner from Chris' grandparents. Finally we were in our own place again. I prayed things would get better but once again Chris' behavior continued and I was always home alone with the baby while he was out partying. I don't even remember a night when we hung out at home by ourselves with our baby as a family. Every night I would sit, anxiously waiting for my husband to walk through the door. I would sing to April in the rocking chair in her dark nursery stumbling on the words sometimes as I found myself simultaneously fantasizing about my husband. Only in my romantic fantasies was Chris excited to be in our company welcoming us into the light with him.

As the weeks rolled by my suspicions of his infidelity began to grow. I felt he was cheating on me although he would always deny it when I confronted him. But he couldn't hide his weird behavior even though he tried his best. The guilt was getting the best of him. Then when I ended up with a sexually transmitted disease he turned everything around and started to accuse me of cheating on him. I knew my suspicions were correct although I had no actual proof. I hadn't cheated so it *had* to be him. On my way to the gynecologist's office I was thinking about how Chris adamantly denied being unfaithful. I wanted desperately to believe him and began to think of any other way I could have possibly contracted the STD. Grasping at straws I remembered using the public restroom at the mall the week before and wondered if it was possible I picked it up there. I asked the doctor and he assured me it wasn't from a public toilet seat. He wrote me a prescription to get filled and I was on my way.

ONE OF CHRIS' HIGH SCHOOL FRIENDS, Mike, was planning a party while his parents were going to be out of town. Chris was talking about it for days. I decided I needed to make a stink about never getting to go out so he would include me and maybe I could get a glimpse into the night life he enjoyed so much when I was at home with our baby. He reluctantly asked if I wanted to go to the party with him to which I answered, "Yes, of course I do" and arranged for my mom to watch April. I decided I was going to go into the evening with an open mind and determined for us to have a fun night. I had to make Chris see we could still have a good time together. I even decided I would have a couple of drinks because I knew it would please him.

Chris introduced me to a few people as we walked through the house to the kitchen looking for Mike. As Chris reached in the fridge, Mike came in from the backyard to refill his drink and saw us. He said he was glad we could make it and even commented on the fact I was there. "How did you talk this guy into finally taking you out?" he asked me as he gave me a welcoming hug and congratulated us on the baby. We both just smiled and Chris gave Mike a playful punch to the gut as he said, "Don't go saying things like that. She'll be expecting to go everywhere with me." They both just chuckled and Mike handed Chris a pill which he immediately popped into his mouth and washed it down with the beer he had just grabbed from the fridge. I asked them what it was and they said it was a Quaalude. Chris told me I should take one because it would relax me. I told him I was relaxed and didn't want one but I would like to have a drink. He mixed me up a screwdriver real quick and we headed out to the backyard. Things seemed to be going good so far with the exception of the pill popping.

A couple hours passed and we were actually having a good time together. Much to my surprise Chris was with me for most of the evening. It felt so good to be out as a couple and feel as though he was happy to be there with me. Later as I chatted at the patio table with some of the girls I glanced at him while he joked with some of the guys on the other side of the pool. He was a fun guy, always trying to make people laugh which made me start remembering part of why I fell in love with him to begin with. The evening filled my heart with hope. We hadn't had a happy night together for quite some time. He looked over and saw me admiring him. He shot me a wink and a smile which gave me goose bumps like a school girl getting her first interested look from a guy. It made me feel as though he still loved me and I believed there was still hope for us.

We reconnected, grabbed another drink and made our way out to the backyard. Chris really seemed to be proud to show me off to his friends and genuinely cared that I was with him. As the night wore on, people were leaving and soon I noticed everyone had left except Chris and I and Mike's girlfriend. I had heard rumors during the party about her being a hooker. It didn't surprise me because Mike was known for such things. Mike was also known for and teased about having the biggest manhood of all the guys in their group of friends.

As I sat on a patio chair by the pool waiting for Chris to come back from the bathroom, I saw Mike and Tracy taking off their clothes while making out heavily. It felt very awkward so I tried to look elsewhere. I kept thinking I wish Chris would hurry up. What was he doing in there? Once naked, they stepped into the pool and continued on the steps. Just as I decided to go find Chris, he finally came out and asked me to go skinny dipping with them.

Apparently the guys discussed it before he went in to the bathroom. I told him I was very self-conscious of my body, I mean, come on. I just had a baby and hadn't lost all the baby weight yet. But I saw they were busy in the shallow end and began to entertain the idea if Chris and I stayed in the deep end. Again, I knew it would please him and I thought the cool water would help sober me up a bit too. After only a couple drinks I felt like I had guzzled an entire 6 pack of beer. I started to wonder if Chris had dropped one of those pills in my last drink. I gave him a why not shoulder shrug so we undressed and I dove in the deep end after him. When I came up I noticed Chris was whispering with Mike, then he swam over to me as Mike and Tracy resumed making out on the pool steps and asked me if he and Mike could swap girls! He tried to coax me with the promise that Mike would be the biggest I would ever have. I was devastated he would even entertain the idea of sharing me with another man, let alone ASK me to do it! I told him, "NO way! I want to leave, right now." Although he was disappointed, he agreed to leave which surprised me. I got out of the pool and started getting dressed while he told Mike it wasn't going to happen. He came over by me, threw his pants on and we went out front to get in the truck. He didn't say a word to me. I had upset him and I was sure I was going to hear about it as soon as he started driving home.

Much to my surprise, Mike and Tracy jumped in the bed of the truck in their underwear as we were pulling away. I asked, "Why are they coming with us?" as I watched them through the small back window throwing on their clothes in a hurry. He said they weren't done partying and we would just pick up at our house. I told him I didn't want to party anymore and wanted to be with him alone for the rest of the night but he wasn't interested in being alone with me. I was so hurt and upset thinking all he cared about right then was to get a piece of the nasty whore in the back of our truck. All the way home he gave me a lecture. He said I always ruin the night which is why he never wants me to go out with him. *I* ruined the night?!?! When he asked me to swap partners for sex, I was so hurt. It cut through my heart like a knife to see my husband had no problem screwing other women and handing me over to another guy with his blessing of a good time. He crushed my fantasy of us having a nice evening and I knew the night was not going to end as I had earlier imagined.

When we got to our house we were all sitting in the living room. Everyone was pretty drunk and I just wanted to go to bed. I felt like the room was spinning which confirmed to me, someone did indeed put something in my last drink. I never felt that way after only a couple of drinks. Mike and Tracy started making out again on the love seat. Chris began to kiss me and started taking off my shirt while trying to direct me to the couch. I looked over and saw Mike performing oral sex on Tracy. I just knew they were planning on trying to get me to give in and join their orgy. I pushed Chris away and ran to the bathroom to puke. Afterwards, I crawled into our bed. I was so drowsy I couldn't keep my eyes open. I vaguely remember Chris coming in the room to make sure I was asleep. He never admitted it to me but to this day, I believe they had a three some that night.

Chapter 5

I REMEMBER THE FIRST TIME I left. Ok, I didn't technically leave him I guess. April and I had been visiting at my parents' house while Chris was, of course, out with his friends. He had our only vehicle, our old blue pickup truck we bought for a few hundred bucks. It was late afternoon so I started on our walk home pushing April in the stroller. I walked up the driveway and found Chris, Chuck and a few of their friends standing around discussing how he was going to "break the news to me." Immediately an anxiety attack started to brew within me. "Break what news to me Chris?" I blurted out. I startled them and they jerked around to face me. They all looked like little boys who just got caught with their hand in the cookie jar.

I looked to see if the truck was parked on the street as I realized the driveway was occupied by only them. One by one the guys patted him on the back and told him good luck as they left. "Where's the truck?" I asked as we entered the house and I began to take April out of the stroller. He began to explain they went four wheeling and said the rest was history. "What does that mean?" I inquired. He told me the truck was totaled. He already had it towed and found out there was more damage than the truck was worth. It was gone. I was so disappointed in him again. On top of always being home alone, the constant fights, bailing him out of jail, he had to go and total the truck. It was our only transportation. I felt overwhelmed. I told him I couldn't take it anymore, put the baby back in the stroller and headed back to my parents' house. Chris followed me down the block trying to explain. This in itself was unusual but I didn't want to hear more of his excuses. I just wanted him to stop behaving so irresponsibly and selfishly. I needed him to grow up and be a responsible adult. I stopped and turned around to face him as he pleaded with me to come back home.

It was the first time I actually entertained the idea of really leaving him. I looked down at the stroller and was met by our baby's big beautiful blue eyes. She looked back and forth at us both as if to say "What are we doing here guys?" In the moment, I felt she was far too young to lose her daddy and we owed it to her to keep trying to make it work. In my heart I knew things were not going to change. He had already broken the same promise to change his partying ways so many times but for some reason I just couldn't go through with it. I felt I couldn't give up so easily, so against my better judgment, I turned the stroller around and we walked home together.

We were waiting to hear about Chris getting a settlement for hurting his arm on the job. He hadn't worked in months and things were very tight with only my income and his small workman's comp. checks. After many doctor appointments and tests they concluded he had lost about 10 percent use of his arm and he was to receive a lump sum payment of $8,000.00 through workman's comp. We were so happy when we found out. We discussed the money would be best spent to get the bills caught up and get another vehicle, a family vehicle this time. It couldn't have come at a better time. I finally had a sense of calmness and relief like maybe everything would be ok. This could be a fresh new start for us as a family. Again, he had promised me he was done with partying and he was going to be the husband I deserved and a good father to our baby girl.

I'll never forget the sense of betrayal I felt when he unexpectedly showed up at my work only a few days after I had deposited the check. I was working in the drive-thru of the bank when he drove up on a Harley Davidson motorcycle he informed me he was going to buy with the money. He knew if he broke the news to me while I was busy at work I wouldn't have a chance to dispute it. He would purposely put me on the spot in front of other people when he didn't want me to question his decisions. He knew I wouldn't want to discuss our private affairs with my co-workers listening to everything. I was so embarrassed and so tired of him always putting himself and what he wanted before his family. I was so upset I didn't care who was listening. I questioned him about the promises he had made to me and reminded him of all the bills we said we were going to pay off with the money. I could tell he was getting upset. He didn't like anyone, much less a woman, telling him what to do even though he agreed just days before it was the right thing to do with the money. I asked him if we could discuss it later at home and he told me, "No. The whole reason I'm here is to pick up a check to pay for the bike. I'm on a test drive and the guy is waiting for me." Every time I tried to have a discussion with him about something important like couples do, he would tell me to quit my bitching and get over it. This was his way of saying it again. I entertained the idea of telling him I wasn't going to do the withdrawal but I knew he would just go inside the bank and do it anyway. I felt defeated and had one of my tellers do the transaction. He shot me his usual arrogant smile as he removed the check from the capsule and rode off.

When I got home from work I tried to talk some sense into him but to no avail. He was not going to give it up. I knew a motorcycle was only going to make matters worse. He wanted so bad to fit in with the biker crowd and told me he was going to join a biker gang. He told me he might have to do things as an initiation into the gang, things I might not like. I was curious and asked, "Like what?" He ran down a list which included robbery, assault and of course having sex with whomever they told him to. He also told me sometimes they belittle and degrade you to see how tough you are which I knew he was not about to let happen to him. I kind of chuckled and said, "Yeah, well you will never be in a gang then because I know you won't be having that!"

His motorcycle soon became his baby, his pride and joy. I believed he loved it more than he loved me and his daughter, at least that's how he made it seem. He also loved the fact I had no transportation to go anywhere without him or to go looking for him. He began to think he was invincible. He was a biker now, no one could touch him. And what did I get? Yet another sexually transmitted disease! It made me sick to my stomach to think my husband would rather be having sex with some nasty whores who have sexually transmitted diseases than to be home making love to me. And it used to drive me crazy knowing he was riding those bitches on the back of his motorcycle on *my* seat with their arms around *my* husband! The truth is the nasty whores he was with probably got more time and attention from him than me. I know they rode on my seat of the motorcycle more than I did. I decided it was time to make an appearance at the bars he hung out at, if for nothing else but to show proof of my existence.

IT WAS MY 21ST BIRTHDAY AND Chris couldn't wait to take me out, only because he thought it would be fun to get me drunk. His plan was to go bar hopping which would be the perfect excuse to see what he's doing when he's not with me. Of course we started out at the neighborhood pool hall and bar, Family Billiards, where he and his friends hung out since they were probably 16. He told the bartender/owner it was my 21st birthday and to give me whatever I wanted. I couldn't help but notice the shocked and puzzled look on the owners' face when he asked, "Aren't you two the same age?" I said, "Yes, why?" He then shot Chris a scowl and said, "You've been telling me for a couple of years now that you were older than 21. I knew I should have carded you." Chris just gave him his usual arrogant laugh as he ordered a screwdriver for me, a beer for himself and a couple shots of Yukon Jack whiskey. He gave me one and took the other shot glass, held it up and said, "You have to chug it, Karen. Don't sip it." Oooohhhh, it was terrible. It tasted like Formula 44D cough medicine only a little worse. Then he ordered another round. I had 2 screwdrivers and we each had 2 shots of Yukon Jack. I had to use the restroom and started on my way down stairs. I was definitely feeling a bit lightheaded as I sat on the toilet. I had never had a shot of hard liquor before. I got up, washed my hands and went to open the door except it wouldn't budge. "How could it be locked from the outside?" I asked myself. It couldn't be which means someone is holding the door shut so I can't open it. I figured Chris was messing around with me and told him to let me out. Suddenly the door was free and opened easily. I was sure Chris would be standing there but he was nowhere around the restroom. Through the glass behind the bar I could see he was still on the upper level at the bar with his friends waiting for me. The two guys playing on the pool table in front of the restroom started laughing at me. I asked if they were the ones holding the door shut and they said "Yes, we were just messing around. Are you here alone?" I answered, "No and that wasn't funny" as I swung around and walked away making my way back to my husband. Chris could see I was irritated and asked what was wrong. In hindsight, I probably should have told him nothing because he was so pissed he approached the two guys. They could see he was pissed and knew a fight was about to start. All three of them grabbed pool sticks and started swinging as Chris yelled out to them they should watch who they are messing with. A few of Chris' friends joined in and they fought the guys as they shoved them toward the front door to throw them out. We waited a while then left to head to another bar.

A couple bars later he decided to try a strip club. I think he thought by that time I was drunk enough not to mind. I felt uncomfortable but I wanted to see what it was like. What the women my husband enjoyed looking at so much were like. Chris grabbed a couple chairs at the bar I assumed was his regular spot. Within minutes he had topless women rubbing their little pasty clad breasts on him asking what he wanted to drink. He gave one of them our order and asked her to send the owner over. Much to my surprise, the owner was there within minutes and Chris introduced us. He continued, "What did I tell you? Her tits are much bigger than any of the girls you have in here. My girl would bring you a lot more business." He told me to take my shirt and bra off to audition for the guy. I was horrified! My own husband had been talking to this guy about practically pimping me out! I got up and stormed out! As I started walking down the street Chris came up behind me and grabbed my arm. He said, "All you had to say was you weren't interested." To which I said, "You *knew* I wouldn't be interested! How dare you? I'm your *wife*! Doesn't it mean anything to you? This entire night was a set-up, wasn't it? Making me chug all those drinks and shots, you must have thought if you got me drunk enough, I *just might* agree to do it! Huh? This was never meant to be a birthday celebration for me was it? I could see you had this all planned. You're so selfish. Take me home."

The hot July desert heat and rumble of the Harley stirred the liquor in my belly as the engine surged down Boulder Highway. It was around midnight and no longer my birthday. As Chris pulled up to the house I remember thinking, "Watch him drop me off and leave to go meet up with the guys." Sure enough! Right then it didn't matter to me. I really didn't want to be around him. My heart was so heavy with hurt and betrayal.

APRIL WAS ALREADY A YEAR OLD. We had a wonderful birthday party at the house for her with family and friends. I was so happy Chris stayed home for the whole party and even helped me with all the preparations. I started to wonder if this would be the turning point in which he would start to care more about his family than his partying but didn't want to get my hopes up only to be let down again. I made it a point to thoroughly enjoy the time we had together and not think about what it meant or where we would go from there.

I had lost most of my baby weight but my breasts still had not gone down in size. I had to special order bras which were very expensive. I couldn't find a size 32I in any store. I was tired of being in so much pain from carrying around my enormous breasts so I decided to have the breast reduction. Of course Chris was against it and we all know it wasn't because he was worried about me having surgery. He made some insulting comments about how was he supposed to get turned on by having to look at my stitched up tits. It was always about him but he wasn't the one in pain from them, I was and I wasn't going to let him discourage me because I knew I would feel so much better. I explained to him my petite frame was much too small to support the weight of the huge breasts. I was in constant back and neck pain. I told him I was going to make an appointment with a plastic surgeon for a consultation and to see what the procedure entailed. He wasn't happy with my decision to go through with it but I told him he had no problem doing whatever he wanted to do if it made him happy, so it was my turn to do something for me.

I was informed by the surgeon I would have to go off the birth control pill as it affects the hormones and it would need to be out of my system for at least a month prior to surgery. He also said I would need to buy a certain bra in my new size, a 32C, he would put on me immediately after surgery. Then he began to talk about the cost and told me to check with my medical insurance company because most of them didn't cover the whole cost even if it was declared medically necessary. Suddenly my thoughts shifted to the finances. Chris had spent the whole check he received on his motorcycle and accessories so we had nothing in savings but I was determined to have the surgery and decided I would see if my bank would give me a loan for the portion I needed to pay.

I saw my gynecologist regarding another form of birth control. I had been taking the pill since

The Haunting Sliver of Light

April was born and much to my surprise, the doctor told me I would be just fine without any birth control since the pill was in my system for a year. I was a little taken back by his response but who am I to question a doctor? I was only 21 years old, what did I know? It was the first time I ever used birth control so I had to rely on his expertise. As we concluded our visit he told me good luck and I went on my way.

I got the loan from my bank and had the surgery. Everything went well. I was a C cup and felt light as a feather. I gained back the confidence in my appearance again, was more proportioned and didn't look like a freak anymore but best of all, my back and neck pain were gone. However, my husband began to treat me as though I wasn't a "whole woman" anymore. When we did make love he couldn't even bring himself to look at them let alone touch them. Sometimes he even told me to leave my bra on because it would be easier for him to get aroused if he didn't have to look at them. Almost everything that came out of his mouth directed toward me was belittling and degrading. He didn't want me to have an opinion of my own, let alone act on it without his approval. Which was why he reminded me often it wasn't his idea for me to have the surgery so it was my fault he was treating me different and was turned off by the look of my new breasts.

A couple of weeks after the surgery, I realized I was pregnant again. Damn doctor! I got pregnant within the month before surgery. I was scheduled to see the surgeon to have my stitches taken out and was dreading having to tell him I was pregnant so soon after the surgery. I was so nervous he was going to tell me the surgery was for nothing since I was pregnant again. He removed the stitches and said, "Now don't go getting pregnant for a while yet." I burst into tears and told him I was already pregnant and what the gynecologist told me. He was upset to say the least. He said the gynecologist should have known better. I replied, "Yeah, that's what I thought but he assured me I was protected for the month." He patted me on the back and said, "Nothing you can do about it now kiddo. Let's just see how it goes. Maybe the breasts won't grow so much with this pregnancy since so much skin was removed." I wiped the tears streaming down my face with the tissue he handed me and got dressed.

CHRIS FINALLY GOT A JOB BUT it wouldn't last long. His tremendous ego and arrogant attitude got him into more fights than I can count. We got evicted from the house and he decided we would move in with our friend Heather. She had her own apartment and had just had a baby girl who was about 3 months old. He made an arrangement with Heather for me to babysit for her while she worked in exchange for rent. I wasn't happy with it but I really didn't want my parents to know we were evicted. I kind of made them think we were moving in with a friend to share the rent but I hated living there. I was working all day while Chris was looking for a job then he was out partying all night while Heather was working her corner downtown. It made me sick. I knew we couldn't afford our own place on just my salary but we had to do something. After a few months of living with Heather I tried to talk to my husband about our situation. I told him I wasn't comfortable watching Heather's child while she was selling her body. I know I was only babysitting in exchange for rent but I didn't want to live like that anymore. I wanted us to have our own place again. He told me he got a job and decided we would move back in with his grandparents just long enough to save the money to get our own place.

During my fifth month of pregnancy, Chris lost his job again. I started to think we were also going to be living with his grandparents when our second child was born. He swore to me he was out looking for a job every day while I was at work but no one ever called him. My husband was away from me more than he was with me and I began to realize I didn't know if I could believe half of what he told me anymore.

Then early one morning I woke to a light knock on our bedroom door. It was my mother. She came over to tell me my Grandma Clare, my paternal grandmother had passed away. She had been battling cancer for about 6 months and was put in the hospital for her last couple of weeks. My parents were on their way to the funeral home to make arrangements for her to be sent to Chicago for burial. I told her I would get up and meet them at the house later. She nodded her head yes and closed the door.

At the house, everyone was talking about the dates they had to take off work and what flight they should book when I suddenly thought, I wonder if I can even fly right now being so far along. I called the doctor and she said it was too late in my pregnancy to fly on a plane so I informed my parents I wouldn't be able to attend my grandmothers' funeral. I felt bad for my dad but truth be known, I was not heartbroken. Grandma Clare and I had never really been close. In fact, most of my life we were at odds with each other. She and my grandfather separated when I was about 1 year old and she moved in with us. Throughout my childhood she was physically and emotionally abusive toward me and my little brother born with Downs Syndrome, Kevin. I wondered my whole childhood whether my grandmother loved me and what I ever did to make her be so mean to me. But that's a whole other story.

CHRIS WAS NOT HAVING ANY LUCK finding a job and decided he wanted to go to truck driving school.

He told me there wasn't a school in Las Vegas. The closest one was in California, close to his parents' house so he would stay with them as not to have any added expenses. Apparently he had been thinking about it and planning for quite some time. Again, there was no discussion with his wife. It was going to be what he wanted no questions asked but I didn't want him to be on the road. I wanted my husband home with me and our baby especially with another one on the way but he didn't want to hear my disagreement. He told me to ask my parents if April and I could move in with them while he was gone for the three months it took for the schooling. I knew there was no talking him out of it and felt defeated once again. God forbid he was a man about it and went *with* me to discuss it with my parents, as a couple. My parents were not very happy with Chris' idea but of course agreed. Within a week we were getting settled at my parents' house when my dad tried to talk to Chris. He told him a career on the road is no life for a man with a family. He had first-hand knowledge of it since his father was a truck driver. He told Chris some stories of his childhood. How he was away from his father for months at a time and how hard it was but Chris had his mind made up. He never took anyone's advice or even thought about it. It was always his way or the highway. It was so frustrating being married to such an arrogant young man who thought he knew everything and cared nothing about what I felt.

Karen Rowland

It was only a few days before my husband took off on his new adventure. I was happy for him to grow as a person and learn new things however I couldn't help but worry about how the distance between us was going to affect our marriage and family. We were by no means on solid ground with a secure relationship and it only added more doubt in my mind.

The month after Chris left I lost my job. I went into work as usual and my boss, the Assistant Vice President of Savings, took me into an empty office to talk. She explained there were changes coming and I was to train one of the teller trainees to take my job as drive-thru supervisor so my only responsibility would be the position as her secretary/stenographer. I was shocked because it took me 3 years of hard work to be eligible for the position of supervisor. She told me she understood and she was sorry but the orders came from her boss and there was nothing she could do about it. I was upset to say the least. It was also a very emotional time with my husband being gone, the constant worry of his infidelity, living with my parents again, not to mention the crazy hormones being 6 months pregnant. I felt I needed to stand my ground and told her I refuse to train a trainee to take my job as supervisor. She begged me to change my mind because her only other option then would be to fire me. I was insulted and felt betrayed as Sheila and I both felt we had a closer relationship than just boss and employee. Her daughter even stood up for me at my wedding. I then blurted out, "You don't have to fire me. I quit." I stood up and walked out. I headed straight for my desk to gather my personal belongings and went on to the personnel office to be discharged. They gave me my final check and I found myself bawling like a baby in the drive-thru of another branch to cash my check. I second guessed my decision all the way home. Then I realized I couldn't change it and would have to live with it. I started thinking of how I was feeling stagnant at the bank for the last 6 months or so and decided it was probably for the best. After I had the baby maybe I would try something different.

During the three months Chris was gone, he only came home a few times for the weekend. After each visit from my husband, I found I had contracted a sexually transmitted disease. My suspicions of his infidelities were finally confirmed to me. I realized I never should have told him about me suspecting I might have contracted the STD's from a public toilet because he ran with it. Every time it happened he would ask me where I used a public restroom. I told him I gave him the benefit of the doubt early on but when I asked my doctor she assured me I didn't get it from a public toilet seat and if I wasn't cheating then it had to be him. Of course he would still deny it every time telling me the doctor must be wrong because he had no symptoms. All the while he was secretly taking a prescription he got from a doctor in California before he even came home to visit. He thought it would be safe for us to have sex since the medicine was in his system but he was wrong.

Near the end of my pregnancy, Chris' biker friend, Sonny, was killed in a car accident. Sonny was always so nice to me and April. He used to tell Chris he should be at home with his wife and daughter, not out partying with the guys. His death was a shock to everyone. Chris was working but would spend the days and nights he was in town, at the cemetery at Sonny's grave, drinking and smoking pot. He would take a drink and pour one on the grave for Sonny. There were several times I went to the cemetery looking for him in the wee hours of the morning. I was so worried because I knew he was always drunk when it was time to drive home. Chris had decided we would name the baby after Sonny. His parents told Chris, Sonny spoke of us often. They were so touched we wanted to honor Sonny by naming the baby after him they decided to give us his Harley-Davidson sportster motorcycle to keep for our new son, Christopher Clarence. We always thought Sonny was his first name but it turned out to be a nickname. Clarence was his real first name. Oh boy, I really didn't like it but I felt I had no choice. I wanted to name my son, Christopher Charles ever since I was in high school fantasizing about having my own family. How ironic, I would marry a guy named Chris and his older brothers' name was Charles. I had picked Christopher Charles because

I thought it sounded like a strong, powerful name and Charles was my dad's middle name too but Chris wasn't having it. It only made him start thinking there was something going on between me and his brother.

WITH ONLY A COUPLE OF WEEKS left of my pregnancy, my husband gave me the CRABS!!! At first I didn't even know what it was. I was only 22 years old and had never experienced any sexual transmitted diseases before my marriage to Chris. This wasn't like the others though, it was very painful. The itching and burning were unbearable. Thinking it was a bad yeast infection or something of that nature, I tried various over-the-counter remedies. I became very concerned when none of them worked. Only a huge glob of Vaseline would give me any relief so I could get some sleep. I was terrified something was really wrong and could affect the baby so I went to see my new doctor. She assured me the baby was fine. However she urged me to talk to my husband about his infidelities. I told her I had and I felt it was useless since all he did was deny it every time I confronted him with it. We had only been married for 2 years and already I lost count of how many times I suspected he cheated. I don't know why I stayed other than I loved him and wanted to keep our family together. I hoped and prayed he would grow out of the partying and cheating and finally see how he was throwing away a beautiful life with his family.

A few days before I gave birth to Christopher, Chris was in a motorcycle accident while riding Sonny's sportster and sprained his ankle. He was drunk so the bike was impounded and he never got it back. It went to auction because we didn't have the money for the impound fees. It wasn't a bad accident but this would be his excuse for not going to see his second child come into the world. "Besides," he added, "I've already gone through that, once was enough." Excuse me? I didn't have time to argue. I was already spotting when I woke up and took the time to take a shower and do my hair and makeup. My contractions were getting stronger and I had no choice but to drive myself. It was obvious to me this baby was not going to take as long as April did. Chris was laying on the floor in the living room watching the television without a care in the world. My mother was furious when I told her he wasn't going and asked to borrow her car. She would never say anything to him no matter how upset or disappointed she was with him. She went to get her keys and said, "You can't drive, you're in labor! I'll take you."

Immediately upon arrival they set me up in a birthing room. I decided to go to a Birthing Center the second time because I wanted to experience the birth all natural. Mom anxiously watched over me through the rest of my labor. After a few more hours the nurse came in the room again to check me and said it would probably take another hour or so and left. But within a few minutes a huge contraction started and I yelled out, "The baby is coming NOW!" The midwife and nurse rushed in and took their positions. Even though I was doing this birth all natural hoping everything was going to go as smooth as my first labor, the birthing center was right next to the hospital April was born in, just in case.

I remember the midwife saying, "I have to cut you, Karen, this is a big baby and I don't want you to tear." I looked over at my mother who was backed up in the corner by the door watching everything from across the tiny room. I asked the midwife if she was going to give me a shot to numb me first and she said, "We don't have time for that. I will do it when you get the next contraction and you bear down. You won't even feel it." Yeah right, I thought immediately as the next contraction reared its ugly head. I put all my might into it hoping she was right. Afterwards I asked, "Why didn't you cut me?" To which she replied, "I already did" and my beautiful baby boy was born. On July 19th, 1982 he came into the world as mom and I watched him take his first breath. The midwife said, "He has the biggest testicles I've ever seen on a newborn baby. He looks like he's 3 months old already." Then she handed the nurse my baby boy. She whisked him away to be bathed and weighed. "He is a healthy 9lbs.and 12oz." the nurse said. Then she handed my precious bundle to my mother so she could take him down the hallway to the pediatrician's office to be circumcised. The midwife sewed me up and left the room. I couldn't wait to tell Chris we had a boy.

Mom came back shortly after the midwife left and went to hand me my precious baby boy when the nurse came in with the phone I asked for. "I'm calling Chris to let him know it's a boy and we'll be home soon. We only have to stay for another hour to make sure everything is fine," I informed mom. I was overjoyed and just knew Chris would be too. Upon hearing the news, he responded with, "I knew it was going to be a boy this time. Pick me up a Big Mac on your way home." He was always so insensitive. He didn't even ask how the labor went or if the baby and I were ok. Don't even ask yourself if I picked him up a Big Mac, you know I did. We slid through the drive thru and headed home. When we got home with the baby, Chris acted like it was no big deal but he was sure glad to see I remembered his Big Mac.

Chapter 6

SOON CHRIS WAS BACK ON THE road. I was doing laundry and went to put his clean socks and underwear away when I found a pill bottle stashed in the back of the drawer. I opened it, poured them out into my hand and noticed they all had an X across the top but nothing else. I thought, these must be the caffeine pills he told me he was taking to stay awake on the road. Then I remembered he told me they also suppress the appetite and suggested I take them to lose my baby weight. I popped one in my mouth and continued with the laundry while the children were still napping. A short while later my head began to pound something fierce. I tried to lay down hoping it would subside but it didn't work. After another 30 minutes or so of tossing and turning I heard the dryer buzzer and went to fold the clothes. The pounding wasn't letting up so I thought maybe I should drink some water to flush the pill out of my system. I was beginning to get scared and wished I had never taken it. "God, please make it stop," I begged, holding my head in my hands as I applied pressure on my temples. Another hour and 3 glasses of water later, it finally started to ease up. Thank God. I needed to tell Chris what happened when he comes back home. I didn't know if it was because I was so much smaller than him that it affected us differently or if it was because I just had a baby and my hormones were all messed up. I'm just glad it finally stopped because I was ready to go to the hospital. I would have been really embarrassed to tell the doctor I had taken a pill without knowing exactly what it was. I promised myself I would never do that again.

APRIL TURNED 2 YEARS OLD THE September after Christopher was born and my parents decided to take her to Disneyland. I thought it would give Chris and I some time alone to bond with baby Christopher but as usual Chris had other plans. Of course he figured it was party time. He was so happy he happened to be home the same time my parents would be gone. He wanted me to invite one of my girlfriends over so he could supposedly fix her up with his brother Chuck but when he suggested Gina I knew it was because he liked her. I tried to give him the benefit of the doubt again but my gut told me otherwise. Anyway, we invited her and Chuck over for dinner and a swim.

Everything was going good until after dinner when it was time for me to feed the baby. I went in the bedroom to bring Christopher his bottle. I thought I would introduce him to Gina since he was sleeping when she got to the house but when I walked into the kitchen no one was there. I looked outside in the backyard and there they were all 3 of them naked in the pool. I slid open the patio door just enough to stick my head out and asked what was going on. "We're waiting for you to go skinny dipping with us," my husband said. I was so upset and hurt but I just closed the door and went to sit in the dark living room. It always calmed me when I rocked and fed my babies. Now I was hoping Christopher would go right back to sleep so I could address the issue at hand. I began to rehearse what I wanted to say in my head.

Are you kidding me? I just had a baby! I don't even want *you* to see me naked right now you idiot! Why would you think I would want ANYONE ELSE to see me naked? Why would you want your brother to see your wife naked? Not to mention, what makes you think I want my husband to be naked with another woman, a friend of mine? In every aspect, it's so disrespectful to me, our marriage *and* our family! Why is that so hard for him to understand? Aaaahhh!! He infuriated me some times! The truth is he was such a selfish prick and he never took anyone else's feelings into consideration, not even his wife's. I was his wife on paper but he certainly didn't consider me an equal partner in the marriage. My opinion meant nothing to him. He always did whatever he wanted but, believe you me, there were so many limitations on what I was *allowed* to do. Deep down I knew it was bullshit but he was wearing me down. I felt kept. Was he right when he told me I would never be able to make it on my own with two babies? I had begun to feel like a possession of his more than anything. He treated me as though I was beneath him. I was there for sex, cooking, cleaning and raising the children as far as he was concerned. He told me he didn't want me to go back to work either. At first I looked at it as a good sign. He wanted to take the role of husband, father and provider for his family seriously and he wanted me to be a stay at home mom who was always there for our children. But in that moment I was feeling differently. I started recapping our entire marriage in my head as I outlined every beautiful inch of my baby boys' face while he fed and slowly began to close his big chocolate brown eyes.

    I laid Christopher back in his crib and asked Chris to come in the house. I began by telling him I wasn't going to go skinny dipping and I couldn't believe he did that without discussing it with me first. I wouldn't get a chance to tell him everything I was just rehearsing in my head. He just got pissed off and went outside to tell Chuck and Gina I wanted them to get out of the pool and leave. He always blamed everything on me. It ruined the whole mood and the night ended abruptly. They got dressed and went their separate ways. Once they were gone he laid into me about embarrassing him and scolded me for being jealous. After his rant I tried to get a word in shouting, "You're DAMN RIGHT I was hurt and upset my husband wanted to get naked with another woman, AGAIN!" I took a deep breath to keep going and get it all out when he flipped me off, turned around and went to bed. Of course there would be no discussion. He knew I wasn't about to continue the argument in the bedroom so close to our sleeping infant. It was how he always dealt with our disagreements. I was so frustrated I just went in the kitchen to clean up. I don't believe I ever talked to Gina again.

It was obvious Chris had no intention of bonding with his son, just like with April. He would never feed him, change his diaper and very seldom even held him. It was very emotional and I couldn't wait for my parents and April to come home.

Living with my parents was taking a toll on everyone. Everyone could see how disrespectfully my husband treated me and how little he helped me with the children. I'm sure it was very hard for them to even have us all there let alone have to witness how selfish my husband was and watch me tolerate it. My mother told me we needed a place of our own to try and work things out, so I told Chris we had to move. It wasn't long before we found a cute, cozy two bedroom apartment down the street from the UNLV, not far from my family and Chris' grandparents. I prayed it would be the beginning of a fresh start for a happier life. Little did I know at the time, it would be the beginning of the end of our marriage.

BY THIS TIME, CHRIS HAD MOVED on from those silly cross top pills and was snorting crystal meth. He said he needed it to stay awake on the road. He told me the cross tops didn't do anything for him anymore as his body built up a resistance to them so he needed something stronger. Although I didn't believe him, I could do nothing about it. I tried to understand but I believed he was just making up excuses to do drugs. I had suspected he had been snorting meth for quite some time and had just hid it from me. His paranoia was growing and he insisted on leaving his gun with me for protection when he went on the road.

I'll never forget the time he left really late at night after the children and I were already asleep. Unbeknownst to me, he had left the loaded gun right above my head on the lowest shelf of the headboard of our bed. April was the first one up the next morning. She always came looking for me as soon as she woke up and climbed in my bed. She spotted the gun and picked it up. I woke up and opened my eyes when I heard her making a pretend shooting sound and found the gun pointed right between my eyes! I was shaking with fear inside while trying to stay cool thinking she may accidentally shoot me as I noticed her tiny middle finger on the trigger. I took a deep breath and tried to calmly persuade her to give me the gun. She did what I told her and all was fine but I was furious with Chris for leaving the loaded gun within reach of the children. Most of the time, I just didn't know what he was thinking anymore.

Upon his return home, I told him what happened and the only way he could have a gun in the house was if he kept it up high on the shelf in the closet. He just chuckled and said, "You must have been ready to shit yourself." Everything was a joke to him and he never saw the seriousness of anything I was trying to make a point about. It was useless to take it any further. I ended the conversation by telling him to take the gun with him on the road again. I didn't even want it in the house.

He had tormented and ridiculed me for months for not being able to lose those last 20 pounds after having our son Christopher. He also pestered me every day about how fast I would lose the weight if I would just try crystal meth. I think he thought if he could get me to do it too I wouldn't complain anymore about him doing it. He said it wouldn't make me high and feel out of control, it would just give me energy and suppress my appetite.

I remember the first time I tried it. I was so scared. We went to a New Year's Eve party at his friend Dave's house. There was a band playing in the backyard and the house and yard were both packed. We made our way to the kitchen to get a drink. After a while of small talk with some of the guys, Chris tried to get me to flash the guys my breasts but I wouldn't do it. I think he wanted his friends to see what my Frankentits, as he called them, looked like. He was dying for someone else to agree with him and ask how he could be turned on looking at such a sight. He would always tell his friends how bad my scars looked. I got embarrassed and told him to stop being such a dick. Then he pulled a little bottle out of his pocket and suggested I take a pill he said was a downer, to relax me. I told him no but he broke it in half, swallowed one half and shoved the other half in my mouth followed immediately by my drink he forced down my throat . He held the glass tightly to my mouth with his other hand behind my head and just poured it in. I had no choice but to swallow it. I was pissed trying to push his hand away but he just laughed then handed the glass back to me and walked away.

I was embarrassed and very anxious not knowing what to expect. How dare he just leave me when he knows I've never done drugs before and would be scared of how it would affect me? I just stayed in the same spot for a while waiting to start feeling the effects. I didn't know what I was going to experience but I remembered Chris said it would relax me. So I tried to calm myself and just look around the room and focus on what was going on around me. Of course a bunch of people were looking at me since they saw what just happened. I remember wondering if everyone was watching to laugh at me once the pill kicked in. Was I going to make a fool of myself? Stop, just relax, I told myself. I started talking with a couple of older women (probably in their late 40's) for a bit. They started to tell me all about their biker life on the highway. I just listened as I started to feel my eyes getting droopy. Soon I was transported to their world and forgot about everything else. I was day dreaming of being on the back of a motorcycle with the wind blowing through my hair as we rode across the hot desert. Suddenly, I was jolted back to reality by bellowing laughter from the 2 gals. I felt like I had taken a nap. What the hell? What time is it? How long was I sitting there? I had to find Chris.

I began to work my way to the backyard searching for my husband and a clock. Then I heard someone say it was only a minute before midnight. I tried to hurry so I could be with my husband at the stroke of midnight but as I got to the back door everyone started counting down so I stopped and waited. My eyes searched through the crowd and I spotted him in the backyard with his arm around one of the neighborhood tramps as they sat on the trunk of an old car. He was kissing her as his free hand took turns groping her breast and rubbing her crotch. I couldn't believe what I was seeing. My heart was breaking and my eyes started to well up with tears. When I turned away I saw my brother-in-law, Chuck standing right next to me. He also saw what my husband was doing and could tell I was devastated. He leaned over to kiss me as everyone yelled out "Happy New Year"! I turned my head so he would kiss me on the cheek then pushed my way through the crowd in the yard. I wiped the tears streaming down my face as I felt my hurt turn to anger. I stomped right up to Chris demanding to go home. He knew by my reaction I saw what he was doing with her and told me I was over-reacting. With his usual degrading sarcasm and arrogance he made it clear to me and everyone around us, he would not be taking orders from a woman. "Go if you want, I'm not leaving. The night is young" he said. To which I replied, "Fine. I'll just walk home" and started on my way to the front yard. I thought, "You want to be an asshole? I will call your bluff." I knew I wouldn't even get to the sidewalk out front before one of the guys came to offer me a ride home and Chris knew it too. He knew even though he didn't treat me good he sure didn't want any other guy around me. I was only about 5 or 6 feet from him when he came trotting up to catch me. "Alright, alright, we'll go home." he said. "But you know you're being a real bitch right now right?" All I could say was "Yep, it's always me." We jumped on the Harley and he sped off. Here we go. All the way home I knew he was conjuring up a scheme to make it my fault. I couldn't wait to hear how he was going to spin this one.

The Haunting Sliver of Light

As soon as we walked through the door he started a tantrum because I ruined his night. I cut the night short by being jealous. "It was only a kiss" he said so arrogantly. "Are you kidding me? I saw everything! It *wasn't* just a kiss and she's not your WIFE!" I yelled. I was tired and didn't want things to get any uglier. I just wanted to go to bed but he said I owed him for ruining the night which meant he wanted sex. It was so obvious his dick was throbbing for HER and he wanted me to finish the deed. It made me sick.

He could see I was ready for bed so he laid out a very small line of crystal meth on his cloudy mirror and said he wanted me to do it. He told me it wasn't going to hurt me. He said it was only a little to keep me awake long enough to make love. How dare he call it "making love"? He just wants me to satisfy him since he got all worked up with the whore. I sat there staring at the tiny bit of white powder while he went to take a shower. I was really scared but then I started thinking of how many times he had done it and a whole lot more than what he laid out for me. I began to wonder, "How bad could it be? Surely one time wouldn't kill me." I knew if I didn't do it he would have me up all night badgering and tormenting me. And besides, by this time, Chris didn't care if I wanted sex or not. If he wanted it we were going to have it. He told me a wife isn't supposed to say no when her husband wants sex. It was always too rough when he forced me. I knew I would be hurting in the morning if I didn't give in. When he came back in the living room he noticed the meth was gone and asked if I did it or threw it away. He beamed from ear to ear like he should have when our babies were born, so proud yet arrogantly, knowing he got his way when I said I did it. Problem was, after sex I couldn't go to sleep. I was up all night, cleaning. Damn it, he was right. I didn't feel high at all but I had a burst of energy. I had no appetite either which made me think maybe he's right about it helping me lose the weight. I began to think maybe I *should* try it.

It was also the New Year's Eve Chuck was in a terrible accident with their childhood friend, Joe, who lived across the street from him. Grandpa McGaughey called us in the morning and told us Chuck was in the hospital. He left the party right after us and when he got home Joe was in front of his house wiping down his car. He wanted to take Chuck for a ride in his new sports car. Chuck wasn't ready for the night to end so off they went. Joe drove out of the city and soon they were on a lonely, dark road out in the desert. Joe was speeding up bragging about how fast the car could go when he misjudged a turn in the road. Suddenly the car flipped, turning over and over a few times as it roared out into the desert. Joe was thrown from the car, hit his head on a boulder upon landing and was killed instantly. Chuck found himself paralyzed from the waist down after coming to. He was kind of pinned in the vehicle and had to wiggle out of it. He called out for Joe but there was no response. He called out several more times with a growing panic in his voice each time but he never got a response. It was clear to him Joe was either dead or unconscious.

Either way he was going to have to drag himself by his arms out of the desert and back to the road to flag down a vehicle for help. He looked around to get his bearings and figure out which way the road was but all he saw was an infinite sea of darkness. He listened for the sound of a vehicle on the road to guide his direction. He listened and he listened then he finally thought he saw a faint light, maybe the headlights of a car. In a few seconds he noticed the lights were getting bigger and brighter. He was right. He knew which way to head and estimated he was probably a hundred yards from the road. It was a good thing Chuck was a big stocky guy, very fit and in shape from lifting weights. He had strong arms and would have to rely on them and only them to get him and Joe some help. He stretched his arms out and pulled himself forward hauling his motionless bottom half, over and over and over again until he finally reached the road. All he could do was wait and pray a car came along soon. He was in pretty bad shape and worried about Joe's fate. Thank God it wasn't long before someone came and he was taken to the hospital.

I called my mom to tell her what happened to Chuck and ask if she could keep the children a little longer so we could go to the hospital. I remember walking in to the hospital emergency room with Chris. The nurse at the desk buzzed us in. As we walked down the hall we anxiously checked every bed looking for Chuck. We were glad to find him coherent but he was all bloody and pretty torn up. I don't know when he learned of Joe's death but he already knew when we showed up. The first thing he blurted out was, "Joe's dead! He frickin lost control of the car and we frickin went flying out into the desert. Oh man, I can't feel anything below my waist! I'm frickin scared man!" I had never seen Chuck so vulnerable. He looked defeated and humiliated. This big, strong young man was laying there helpless as a baby. It was so emotional. My heart was breaking for him as I felt his pain. I involuntarily started to cry. All I could think was who was going to care for him when he went home? Grandma and Grandpa McGaughey were too old to be his caregivers, they needed looking after themselves. He told us the doctors already told him he would be in the hospital for a while. They had lots of tests to do and would then determine if they would be able to operate to correct the paralysis.

After a few months, a couple of surgeries and some physical therapy he was released and sent home to heal. There was no more paralysis, his prognosis was good and the doctors believed he would be able to walk on his own again. I talked to Chris and offered for Chuck to move in with us for a while to recuperate. After all, this is my husband's brother. Who else is going to look after him? I loved him like a brother and felt it was the right thing to do. Chris knew Grandma and Grandpa McGaughey couldn't take care of him so he reluctantly agreed I would look after Chuck.

While Chris went to get Chuck I cleared the coffee table to make room for his medications and medical supplies. I got a pillow and blanket from the closet, set them on the arm of the couch and played with the children waiting for them to arrive. I was hoping Chris would see how much I loved him by graciously taking care of his brother but it would only last a couple of weeks because Chris was too jealous. He hated leaving town with a load knowing it would leave me and Chuck alone for days at a time. He didn't like me fussing over Chuck as he put it. I was only trying to give his brother the best care I knew how but he was so ungrateful and always saw an ulterior motive in everything I did or said. It only fed his suspicions of Chuck and I having sex which wasn't true. His distrust was all driven by the guilt of his own infidelities and deceit.

Chris' erratic behavior was noticeably increasing. Chuck and I talked about it after he left with his load. He told me none of their childhood friends even wanted to hang out with Chris anymore because he was getting too deep into the drugs and was too paranoid of everything. I learned Chris was accusing all their childhood friends of sleeping with me and would argue with them about it on a regular basis. They had all had enough of it. Chuck knew who Chris' main connection was and suggested we go together to tell him not to sell to Chris anymore. I was ready to try anything, so we did but to no avail. He laughed in our faces and insisted he would sell to whom ever had the money. It was none of his concern if someone let themselves get addicted, he didn't care. In fact, he hoped they *did*. It would ensure him another longtime customer. Chuck and I looked at each other in disbelief. We thought he would cooperate with us since Chris was his friend. We hoped he cared about what the drugs were doing to Chris and our family but we were wrong. We left and Chuck suggested we come up with an alternate plan. "Well, it was worth a try," he said as I drove to my mom's house to pick up the children.

Chuck was healing well and getting around good with little to no assistance. When Chris came home and saw Chuck on his feet in the kitchen helping me cook dinner, he made up his mind he had to go. He told his brother it looked like he was able to look after himself so he would take him home after dinner. Once we cleared the table and finished the dishes, we packed up Chucks' stuff. He gave me a big hug as he thanked me for everything and whispered in my ear, "It's going to be alright. I'll be in touch."

Once Chuck was gone my husband asked me if I was ready to try things his way to lose the rest of my baby weight. I was desperate to please him so I agreed. It became routine when Chris was in town, to lay me out a tiny, little line in the morning after I had breakfast with the children. I couldn't tolerate the horrible taste in the nasal drainage so I started putting it in my breakfast tea. I would go the rest of the day without eating. Wow! I couldn't believe it. I got the cleaning at our apartment done and still had energy to go over to Grandma and Grandpa McGaugheys' house to clean for them too while they visited with the children. Then I would help Grandma McGaughey make their dinner before we would head home. It was the least I could do for them since they were letting us use their car. Grandpa McGaughey now 90 years old didn't like the fact he couldn't see good enough anymore to drive but they loved seeing the children almost every day.

After just a couple months, I had lost those 20 pounds and then some. Chris controlled it the whole time. I remember one day we were in bed after having sex and he was holding me from behind. He said I was getting too skinny and told me I couldn't have anymore. I was fine with it since I had accomplished the weight loss I hoped for. I was only using it to lose weight in the hopes my husband would think I was attractive again. I was desperate to keep my marriage and family together and get my husband back from the dark world that was sucking him in. I had thought maybe if I was also doing the drugs I would be able to better understand where he was coming from and lose weight too. I had tried everything else. It was my last hope of helping him and keeping our family together. Then I realized he finally got me to break. I gave in when I said I never would. Now he will hold it over my head and use it to control me. I was very naïve. A mere 22 years old with two small children. I never did drugs before so I didn't know anything about them. All my drug education came from Chris and he only told me what he wanted me to know. And it sure wasn't the truth about the dangers of drug use. Looking back, I don't think he was even aware of all the dangers himself and what it was going to do to us.

Chapter 7

WITHIN A COUPLE DAYS, CHRIS STARTED on his way to California again with another load. Shortly after he left the phone rang. It was Chuck calling to tell us their mother was in the hospital. "Oh no, is she alright?" I inquired. He explained she went to the restroom at work and her heart skipped a beat causing her to faint. Falling to the floor, she hit her head on the toilet and went into a coma. He was calling to see if he and Chris could drive there together. I told him Chris had just left about 30 minutes earlier with a load. He asked if he was on his way back to California and I said yes. He said if he left right away he might be able to catch up to him and asked me if I thought my mom would watch the children so I could go too. I told him I would ask her and get right back to him. I wanted to be there for my husband and his family so I called my mother and explained what happened. I asked if she could keep the children for a few days and she agreed. After I called Chuck back I hurried up and packed a bag for the children and one for myself. I dropped the children off at mom's house and hurried over to Grandma and Grandpa McGaugheys'. I figured I should leave their car there for them since Chuck wouldn't be home to get what they might need at the store. We jumped in Chuck's white mustang and headed for the freeway.

We hoped we would be able to catch up with Chris since he hadn't left too long before us. When we did catch up with him, he was furious to see Chuck and me together. In his mind it only confirmed his suspicions there was something going on between us. We told him we had just received word his mother was in the hospital in a coma and were trying to find him on our way. I tried to explain I wanted to be there to support and comfort him and my in-laws but he once again made it out to be something devious. I told him we didn't have time to argue and I would ride with him in the truck the rest of the way thinking it would make him feel better. I could tell his mind was racing so I tried to reassure him. "If something was going on between me and Chuck do you really think we would have been looking for you?" I asked. He hardly said two words to me so I just kept my mouth shut the rest of the way and let him think about it.

When we got to the hospital we quickly found their dad and two younger brothers, Kelly and

Steven. Understandably, they were beside themselves pacing the hall outside June's room. The three of us went in to see her. She was hooked up to machines and was laying there lifeless. She looked as though she was already gone. I took her hand and said a prayer while Chris and Chuck went out into the hall to talk to their dad and find out what her prognosis was. I left the room to join them reaching out for my husband. He reluctantly put his arm around me. I hugged him tight. Just then the doctor returned after reading the results of her brain scan. He informed us she was brain-dead. The boys went crazy! They started yelling and screaming, "No, this can't be happening! Isn't there anything you can do?" But the doctor explained once the brain is dead it's over and there was absolutely no activity. He told us the machine was breathing for her and she was basically already gone. We all collapsed into each other's arms and began to weep. Following the doctor's advice, my father-in-law reluctantly agreed to take her off life support. With us all standing around her bed for comfort, the doctor unplugged the breathing machine. The monitor offered a continuous beep and displayed a solid straight line within a minute. She was gone and everyone was devastated. What a freak accident! It was only a couple of months before during a physical for work she was given a clean bill of health. We went back home and June was quickly waked and buried in Las Vegas about a week later. She was only 42 years old.

The elder of Chris' younger brothers, Kelly, had just come home from the Army a few months prior to their mother's death. He was discouraged and devastated as were we all. He decided to move to Las Vegas to start fresh and asked Chris if he could stay with us. Kelly was not a threat to Chris and I believe he thought Kelly would be the perfect snitch. He was certain Kelly would tell him everything that happened while he was out of town in the hopes of catching me in the act of one of the many things he always accused me of. What he didn't realize was Kelly wasn't like him. He wasn't arrogant, controlling and selfish. Kelly was a kind and caring person and it didn't take long before he saw how terrible my husband treated me. He was busy looking for a job during the day and in the evenings we would have dinner with the children and heart-to-heart talks after they were tucked in.

Kelly didn't go out partying or looking for a female. He was home with me and the children every night. It was as if he felt a responsibility to look after the children and I while his brother was gone. I truly didn't feel he was doing it because Chris had told him to. When I thanked him for it he said, "It's the least I can do for you and Chris letting me stay with you. Besides, it's my pleasure. I enjoy our time together and I like that we are getting to know each other better too."

Within the first couple of weeks, Kelly witnessed Chris accuse me of all sorts of things he had conjured up in his mind while he was on the road. He tried to tell his brother he knew I hadn't done any of what he was accusing me of but it only made Chris start doubting Kelly's loyalty, which in turn solidified his belief of not letting another man into our home and personal affairs for fear of losing me to him. Deep down I believe he knew he wasn't being a good loving husband and father. He knew most guys would love to have a good woman and 2 beautiful children to come home to. I knew several of his friends told him so themselves. He knew he was wrong but he was too proud and selfish to admit it. Then he would have to change which wasn't an option for him. He wanted his cake and to eat it too. He wanted his family but he wanted years to be able to play before honoring his marital commitments. He expected me to just deal with his cheating and partying ways. With his increasing drug use his anger and dominance grew. There were several times Kelly came to my rescue pulling my husband off of me and telling him he shouldn't be treating me in such a way. I hated that Kelly was in the middle but truth be known I was thanking God he *was* there.

After another argument, Chris left town again. I was visibly upset which prompted Kelly to console me. I could tell he genuinely felt bad for me. He told me he would never treat me the way Chris did if I was his wife and said he wanted to marry me and help me raise the children. What?! I couldn't believe what I was hearing. I didn't realize he had started to develop feelings for me. Or was it just the "knight in shining armor" syndrome? Kelly was one of the sweetest guys I had ever met. I believe he wanted to rescue me and the children from the controlled existence we had come to know as our own. Either way, I assured Kelly while I appreciated his offer came from the heart, it would never be. I loved him as a brother and nothing more. We agreed never to tell anyone of his proposal.

Job prospects were looking bleak for Kelly and he couldn't stand to see how his brother treated me so he decided to go back to California. Once we were alone again, Chris' hostility was allowed to fester. As the weeks passed, all of his childhood friends stopped coming over. They could see he had crossed over the line and we were in a deep dark hole. Only crack heads and their whores were in Chris' new circle of friends. I desperately tried to make my husband understand there was no chance of our marriage surviving if he was going to keep drugs and the partying as part of our lives. However, his behavior continued. His temper and use of drugs had grown. He thought nothing of pushing me out of his way and shoving me into the furniture and the walls when he saw fit. I found myself trying to avoid talking to him for any reason. This monster he had become had my husbands' appearance but he was not at all the man I married anymore. I realized I had become afraid of him. Chris' next load out of town couldn't come too soon. I waited with bated breath.

The Haunting Sliver of Light

This time he would be gone for four days and I would get some peace at last. I decided to do some spring cleaning and have a yard sale when he got back. The kids had outgrown so many clothes and since my husband insisted I not go back to work after Christopher was born, I didn't need my dresses and heels anymore. I got a chair and climbed up to reach some boxes of shoes on the shelf in my closet. After setting aside several pairs of high heels, I opened another box only to gasp at the sight of needles and syringes along with a big baggy full of white powder! My heart sank. I could not believe Chris was shooting up. He always told me he was so against it and even though he was using drugs, he said he would never use a needle, yet another broken promise. I quickly put everything back together in the box and put it back on the shelf as best as I could remember it was. He made it quite clear from the moment I found out he was using crystal meth, if I ever threw it away or flushed it or even touched it, he would be furious and there would be hell to pay. No longer in the mood to sort through things for the yard sale, I set everything aside. I began to wonder how it ever got to this point.

With a day to go before Chris' return, I debated on how to approach my husband about what I had found in the closet. Should I even tell him I found it? Maybe it would be better if I didn't say anything at all. No, I couldn't do that. I felt betrayed and he was getting away with being dishonest about a lot of things. I finally had proof of one of them and I was going to confront him about it. All day I couldn't get it out of my mind. I must have rehearsed a thousand different scenarios, all of them ending the same, with him erupting in rage. It made me anxious and scared but I couldn't just ignore it. I couldn't do it anymore.

THE NEXT DAY WHEN HE CAME home, I still wasn't settled on what I was going to say. Almost as soon as he walked in the door, the phone rang and Chris answered it. It was his youngest brother, Steven, calling to tell us Kelly was killed in an accident. He had been out barhopping with some friends the night before. When he asked his friend to take him home because he was ready to call it a night, his friend told him he was not ready to go so Kelly decided to walk home. He walked for miles in the pouring rain. It was raining so hard he couldn't see 2 feet in front of him. Two blocks from his warm, safe home, Kelly stepped off the curb of the island in order to cross the other lanes of traffic. Just then a car came out of nowhere, struck him and sucked him underneath! He was dragged about 50 feet before the driver stopped to get out and see what all the thumping was about. He didn't even realize he had hit a person. He was appalled at the site of a virtually faceless young man. Kelly's face was unrecognizable! The preacher called 911 immediately.

Steven went on to tell Chris he was sitting on the steps outside the apartment waiting for Kelly to come home when he heard sirens close by. He got a terrible feeling in his gut so he started running in the direction of the sirens until he found the accident. He saw a young man lying in the street with his face already covered. He started looking around the scene and recognized his boots on the lifeless body. He broke down and started yelling, repeatedly, "Is that my brother, is that my brother?" A couple officers came over to him and asked why he thought it was his brother. He pointed to the boots and told the officers they were his and his brother had borrowed them. They asked if he could identify the body and he did. Eighteen year old Steven had just lost his best friend and closest brother. He told Chris, Kelly's face was practically gone! I felt so bad for young Steven to have to go through such a traumatic experience and to have it be the last image he had of his beloved brother.

It was a horrendous time for the whole family as it was only six months after their mother June died. Chris was overwhelmed with sadness and covered his face to weep in his hands. After he told me what happened we grabbed each other and held each other, affectionately, like we used to. It felt so good to be in his arms again. I could feel the love between us was still deep down within him. Although I was trying to console my husband, I could not help but reflect on what I found in the closet. I also was grief stricken, I loved Kelly but

I had to get back to the business at hand. I felt horrible for him and the family but it didn't change anything going on in our household. I knew it wasn't a good time to discuss what I had found but I couldn't help myself. The feeling of betrayal swept over me as I fought to find the words to confront him. I began to back away from him and just blurted out, "So when did you start shooting up? And don't deny it, I found your stash in the closet." His grief immediately turned to anger and he demanded to know if I flushed it. "No," I told him, "but I'm not going to tolerate this. That's it, no more. You promised me you would NEVER use a needle!" I had to know, "how could you let this happen?" He commanded me to shut up and shoved me into the wall as he forced his way to the closet. "Everything better be there bitch," he threatened. The anger was swelling inside him again.

I desperately wanted to tell him I was taking the children and leaving but I could not bear the horror of yet another eruption of rage. He had gotten increasingly violent. His "little pushes" had turned into football blocking forced shoves which sent me flying across the room. He justified it by telling me as long as he didn't ball up his fist and actually punch me, it wasn't considered hitting me. So it also meant it was ok for him to slam my head into the wall or a table whichever was closer. I was terrified of him and the damage he might do. I just couldn't have the children around when he found out I was leaving. I knew if it was done in person it would be another huge scene of rage and violence. For everybody's sake, I would have to deceive him into believing "this too shall pass" in order to secretly sneak out and leave the next time he left town. I knew it would be a while since we had the death and burial of Kelly to deal with first so I began to mentally put together an escape plan. For the time being I would have to do whatever I had to in order to appease him.

Within the week Chris' dad and Steven came to Las Vegas to bury Kelly. He was cremated and placed under his mothers' headstone. Only our immediate family was there, my father-in-law Chuck, Kelly's 3 brothers and me. There was no wake or service. I don't even remember going inside the building. When we arrived, one of the cemetery employees already had my mother-in-laws' headstone moved, ready for Kelly to be added. It was heart breaking to watch my father-in-law get down on his knees, lower the urn and gently lay Kelly to rest with his mother. My heart was heavy as I fought to understand the profound agony he must have been feeling losing a child and so soon after the loss of the love of his life. We all cried and said our own silent prayers for a few minutes and left.

It wasn't long after, Chris told me he had a job interview in California and for some strange reason he wanted me to go with him. I think he could sense I was thinking of leaving him and it was his way of preventing it. The children were going to stay with my parents so my grandma could baby sit during the day while they were at work. We started on our way on his Harley but it was raining so hard he turned around and went back home. He didn't think Grandpa McGaugheys' car would make the trip so he talked me into asking my Aunt Rita and Uncle Ronny if we could borrow one of their cars knowing they were the only people we knew with an extra vehicle. They said it was fine and we went right over. Chris was anxious to go so we made it brief. Uncle Ronny explained a few things about the car and handed me the keys. We thanked them and started on our way to the apartment to drop off the motorcycle. Chris pushed his baby into the living room and we headed for the freeway again in their cute little orange Datsun. This would be the first time I ever saw Chris put a needle in his arm. Trying to justify his needle use he told me he just couldn't snort anymore because his nostrils were all torn up inside and his nose just kept bleeding. That's why he started shooting up.

On the way there, he stopped several times for a fix. I had no choice but to watch. I was scared when I saw he was going to continue driving minutes after injecting himself but there was nothing I could do but pray. I tried to use the time we were driving there to talk to him. He was a captive audience at that point and I reminded him of all the promises we made to each other to make a happy life together. I asked him why he felt the need to use drugs and couldn't he see it was out of control and ruining our lives. But as usual, he spun it around so every broken promise was my fault and I was the one ruining everything because I didn't want him to have any fun. I could see I wasn't going to get anywhere with him so I just stopped talking about it. It was very frustrating and aggravating. It was like he put up this shield around him no one could penetrate. He would never entertain someone else's thoughts or feelings. He was selfishly only concerned with his own. I felt like I could never get through to him, so I sat in silence the rest of the way there.

We finally pulled into the parking lot of a trucking company in the Los Angeles area and were greeted by a tall, rather stocky guy as we entered the lobby. There were no introductions so I assumed my husband already knew him. By this time it wasn't unusual for Chris not to introduce me to another man. He didn't allow me to talk to or even be around other men and told me he believed it was inviting the man to get to know me in every sense of the word. I was always expected to stand at least one step behind him. Of course he said it was for my own "protection" and I wanted to believe him. In hindsight, I see it was really just another piece of the puzzle to maintain control and keep me submissive.

Chris shook the guys' hand and walked off with him. It wasn't even 10 minutes later when I saw them heading back toward me and Chris did not look happy. The only thing he would say about it was, "it's just not going to work out." He could see I was looking for an explanation. You're damn right. Are you kidding me? That's it? We came all this way for 10 minutes and you're not going to tell me what happened?

He grabbed my arm, ushered me toward the door and said, "I'm not discussing this with you Karen." He never gave me an explanation for anything. It was so degrading and insulting. My opinions meant nothing to him. I was supposed to be seen and not heard as far as he was concerned. It was so frustrating and belittling. I started to wonder if it was really a drug pickup and something went wrong. We got in the car and left. For a while we drove in silence although I could see he was deep in thought about something. Maybe how he could blame me for his failed plan.

Once we were out of the city and on the open road he demanded I perform oral sex on him while he was driving. I didn't want to do anything to set him off so I obliged. I had my left hand on the floor behind the drivers' seat to brace myself and when my arm got tired, I would switch positions. This made him think I had cocaine hidden behind the drivers' seat and was putting it on his penis. Where the hell would I have gotten cocaine when I was with him the whole time? He was so irrational and delusional. He spotted an exit and quickly pulled off the road into a small grocery stop with a skuzzy little fleabag motel. He parked the car and demanded I get out so he could check it top to bottom. Even though he came up empty handed he still didn't believe me. He insisted he was right and I had just used it all before he decided to do his search. Little did I know at the time, his belief of me hiding drugs from him would become a new major obsession he couldn't let go. He badgered and belittled me once again making everything my fault. Every time he started ranting my mind would wander off and soon he was just a murmur in the distance.

We made it back to Vegas without any more major issues, picked up the children and went home. I would have to contact Uncle Ronny about returning his car but right then I had more important things to attend to. I had just started to unpack the diaper bag and put the children's clothes away when Chris got a call from his boss asking if he was ready to go back to work. He accepted a load and was to leave the next day. Thank God! I was so relieved. I decided the best thing to do was to leave a letter for him at the yard so he would receive it as soon as he got back to town.

The next morning I wished him a safe trip, the children and I kissed him goodbye then I sat down to write the letter to my husband. In it I explained I cannot live like this any longer. There were too many broken promises from him and the drugs had to stop. I would not come back home with the children until it happened and we would be at my parents' house if he wanted to contact me. I packed a few things for the children and I, filled the diaper bag, put the letter in my purse and we headed to the yard. I was sure he had already left and planned on leaving the letter in the sealed envelope with the receptionist all the drivers had to check in with upon their return. I still had a tiny shred of hope he would read my letter and it would wake him up so to speak. I prayed he would realize it was time to get serious and step up to be the man I hoped he still was deep down inside.

THE NEXT FEW DAYS WHILE CHRIS was gone were unnerving. I was relieved to be away from the misery however, I couldn't help anticipating his reaction to my letter. Upon his return, he called me and threw a fit telling me he could not believe I waited until he left town to leave. I told him I couldn't do it face to face because of his growing hostility and physical abuse. I was too afraid of him. He knew what he had to do if he wanted his family back. It was up to him. He was so mad he just hung up. I figured he would need some time to calm down and think things through. At least I hoped he would but instead he ceased the opportunity to party it up.

A couple of weeks went by without any contact at all. Then he finally called me. He told me how he was treating me was wrong and he wanted the opportunity to change, promising he would quit using drugs if I would just come back home. He said he didn't want to talk about it over the phone and asked if I would come to the apartment to talk with him. I agreed. When I got there I was surprised to see Heather sitting on the couch next to him and a trash can in the middle of the living room. Before I could even ask what was going on, she immediately said there was something for me on the shelf in the hall bathroom and insisted I go get it. As I passed the trash can I glanced inside and was appalled to find our wedding album on top of a bunch of other pictures and some of my clothes. He saw my mouth drop open and said he was going to burn everything! I reached in and grabbed our wedding album telling him the children might want it someday, and continued to the bathroom. Much to my surprise, I found my heart shaped gold ring I had sold to her for $50.00 when we lived with her and needed some cash. It was understood I wanted her to keep it so I could buy it back from her someday. When I asked her why she was giving it back to me she said she just thought it was the right thing to do considering the circumstances. Considering the circumstances? I thought maybe she could see Chris and I were headed for a permanent breakup and decided to give me my ring back in case she never saw me again. It was the only reason that made sense to me. I let her know I didn't have the money to buy it back. She assured me it was ok, so I thanked her and put the ring on my finger it used to occupy. A few minutes later she said her goodbyes and left so Chris and I could discuss things.

It was over a year later when Chris finally confessed to me he had sex with Heather after he received my letter at the yard. A couple days later she had called him for some drugs and he told her I had left with the children. He said he had what she wanted and it was ok to come by. When she went over for her stash they got to talking and she felt bad for him. She hugged him and supposedly one thing led to another and they ended up screwing. It disgusted me seeing as though Heather was a hooker by trade making her living on a corner downtown. I also felt betrayed by her. She was supposed to be my friend and to think of all the effort I put into our friendship trying time after time to talk some sense into her about her choice of work. I was always trying to boost her self-esteem so she would come to believe she was better than selling her body. Chris said it meant nothing, it was just sex. She just caught him at a very emotional moment and it never happened again with her. Suddenly it all made sense. Her guilt got the best of her and she thought if she gave me my ring back it would fix things. Maybe in her juvenile mind it did.

Chapter 8

ALL THESE THOUGHTS AND MEMORIES FLOODED my mind on a daily basis. I was captive in the apartment with only time to think. I wanted our marriage to work but I finally realized he was gone and I couldn't get him off the drugs. It was something he had to do for himself and he didn't want to. At the time, the four short years we were married, seemed like it went on forever. Now it feels like a lifetime ago. It didn't register right then but looking back it hit me. I realized the haunting sliver of light was there all along. I was sitting in the dark waiting for my husband to come home to me our entire marriage. It was larger in the beginning, the door ajar waiting for my new husband to come home as I sat in the dark in the middle of the night pregnant then eventually rocking our firstborn as an infant. From the day we married he was out with the guys partying after work every night. Yes, the sliver of light was larger and warmer back then yet still unsettled. By the time our second child was born it grew smaller, more sinister and cold over the years of his drug use.

As terrible as it may sound, I don't remember even one night Chris and I spent together as a couple doing "normal" things. I do remember worrying where he was every night and what he was doing and who he was with. It drove me crazy. I spent our whole marriage wanting the time and attention he gave to his friends and other women for our family. Isn't that the way it's supposed to be? I know no matter where we lived (and we moved quite a few times in those four years) I was home every night alone with the children while he was partying instead of being with us. I think he married me so I wouldn't "get away." He once told me he married me because he knew I was a "good girl," the kind of woman he wanted for the mother of his children. However he wasn't at all ready to grow up. He wanted the best of both worlds. He was still immature and selfish enough to believe he could do whatever he wanted and I should just accept it. No discussion at all, ever. It had to be his way all the time and he thought I would never leave him once we were married and had children. No matter how he treated us.

The days grew into weeks and the weeks into months without contact from anyone outside of who he let in the apartment. He was holding me and the children hostage. Our families also got tired of all the lame excuses he would make me tell them. Everyone knew we were having serious problems and stayed away. Even his childhood friends quit coming over. I was scared to death of Chris and what he might do next. My heart was breaking as he forced me to watch him slowly destroy not only himself but our family and our life together. His addiction and paranoia had grown to new heights.

Since every search of the apartment revealed nothing but his own stash he thought I must be keeping the drugs he believed I was hiding from him on my person. He began going into the bathroom with me at all times insisting on watching me go to the bathroom and undress to take a shower so he could give me a vaginal AND rectal exam. It was beyond humiliating! Each time I fought to hold back the tears. I knew I had to keep it together for the sake of my children. He even dictated my positions for his so called exams.

First I was to just stand there with my arms straight down while he checked up my nose, in my ears and of course, down my throat. I've always had a very sensitive gag reflex and would often puke before he even got to the worse part. He'd then lift my breasts to check underneath followed by lifting my arms straight up saying, "hold the position." After a while, I actually started mouthing the words with him. By then, every cell in my body had lost any ounce of love for him that may have been left and I cringed as he continued running his hands downward. He peeked in my belly button then turned me toward the wall as he put the toilet seat lid down and sat on it. I sometimes caught a glimpse of his face in the mirror while he was assuming his position for his examination. He always possessed an obvious arrogance and condescending grin. I'm sure he loved the control he felt. Once he was in position, I had to assume mine. With my arms still fully extended I was to spread my legs and bend over forward grabbing and holding my ankles. Every time his fingers entered my body in their quest for drugs, I felt I was being violated by something evil. As long as he did not find any drugs hidden inside of my body, I was allowed to proceed with my shower. At times when he was feeling extra paranoid, he would sit on the toilet and make me keep the curtain open until I was finished. It all disgusted me. My heart yearned for my husband to return and save us from the misery but I had lost all hope of ever seeing him again.

His stories of the little grotesque creatures that lived in our kitchen cabinets were much more than his favorite topic of conversation. In his evil mind he had created the most bizarre scenario I believed I would ever witness. In fits of desperation he would throw himself on the floor. His body was twitching and jerking around as he pulled these imaginary creatures off him and threw them into the living room. He would yell and scream saying they were clawing at him and biting him. These goblins, as he put it, with their fangs and dagger like claws, were attacking him and trying to tear him apart!

In the process of his intense battle, Chris had sustained self-inflicted wounds on his face, neck, arms and chest. These wounds would only justify to him these goblins were indeed REAL! Frozen in horror, I could do nothing but watch which would only give him reason to believe I WAS THEIR LEADER! Why else would I not help free him from these evil creatures? In his distorted mental state, he believed the creatures were my faithful soldiers. He said my "tiny warriors" were summoned by my mere thought of them coming to my rescue. His hallucinations were so vivid I myself could almost see these evil creatures which existed only within his wicked mind.

I WOKE ONE MORNING TO CHRIS grabbing my arm. As he pulled me out of the room I looked back to make sure the children were still sleeping and closed the door on our way out. I could tell he conjured up a plan he was about to let me in on. He had done his research, as he called it, under the cover of darkness so there was less of a chance of being seen. He pushed me down the hall to the kitchen and proceeded to tell me he actually saw the coffins his enemies made for me and the children. He wanted to take me there to show them to me. Up until then, I thought the whole coffin story was just a scare tactic of his. He knew I didn't take it seriously and he was determined to make it real for me. He told me he also overheard them talking about an alternate plan to make some money by kidnapping us and selling us into white slavery. He said, "Tonight I'm taking you there and prove it to you." He always told me someone is less likely to be able to make a positive identification if they saw you in the dark.

All day I tried to keep busy with the children to keep my mind off the coffin viewing. I was still skeptical of this story but kind of intrigued at the same time. I guess I was anxious to put it to rest finally one way or the other. After dinner and the children's bath they were off to bed. He made me leave the children with an entourage member while he took me over to Cicero's house. Cicero was one of Chris' newer friends. One of the ringleaders of the bikers he had started hanging out with when he quit his job and started selling drugs. He was also one of his suppliers. Someone Chris grew to trust which struck me odd when he told me he found out Cicero and his henchmen made the coffins.

On the way there he prepared me. "The coffins are in the back bedroom so we have to be very quiet when we sneak around to the backyard. If someone is home, they might hear or see us. So stay close behind me." he explained. He turned the final corner, slowly pulled over to the curb and turned the car off. He pointed across the street, a few houses down and described the house. I was shaking like a leaf and my mind started racing. Nothing like walking into the lions' den, I thought. After all, this IS the guy who wants us dead, right? That's what he's been saying. Just then a very disturbing thought crossed my mind as we crept up to the side of the house. What if he brought me here as a "peace offering"? Was I even going to make it back home to see my children again? Oh my God, I was terrified!

My heart was pounding as we rounded the corner into the backyard. Right then I didn't care anymore if his coffin story was true or not. I just wanted to get away from there and get back to my babies. I tried to turn around to leave but he grabbed me by my arms and turned me back around. Then he pointed to the crate he already had positioned under the window which was my clue to step up on it. Shaking with fear and anticipation, I grabbed hold of his extended hand and stepped up. I silently prayed the room would be empty as I glanced in the window. To my horror, there they were; three small wooden coffins. One was a small adult size and two tiny child-sized ones. They appeared to be made out of scrap pieces of wood obviously made by an amateur but coffins none the less. My heart was in my throat! Horrified, I jumped down, ran to the car as quietly and fast as possible considering I was running for my life! I flung the car door open and jumped in trying to scrunch down in the seat not to be seen. It felt like I was in a horror movie. I closed and locked the doors. Every hair on my body was standing at attention as I trembled from head to toe. I asked God if I would make it back to my children and began to pray.

I wondered what was taking Chris so long to get to the car. Did they see him and ask what he was doing sneaking around in the back of the house? Where was he? I felt a panic attack setting in. "Deep breaths. In through the nose, out through the mouth, in through the nose, out through the mouth," I told myself. It seemed like an hour before he unlocked the driver door and got in. Right away he glared at me with such malice. The whole ordeal had just empowered him. It was obvious he gained more confidence in his authority and control.

All the way home, in his new heightened level of arrogance, if that was even possible, he drilled in my head what would happen to the children and I if we left our apartment. He was manipulating me to believe he was protecting us from these criminals who wanted us dead. But why do they want US dead? We didn't do anything to them, I thought. "What did you do to them for them to want us dead?" I asked. He explained he had ripped off a supplier of his and had been doing some really bad things over the last year or so. "Breaking into peoples' houses, beating them up and robbing them were some of the nicer things I've done. You don't rip off a supplier and get away with it. Now they want me to pay for it and they think the best way to hurt me is to go after you and the kids," he offered, then said I didn't need to know anymore. I was guessing Cicero was the one he ripped off and I wanted to ask why they didn't just go after him but I didn't dare say what I was thinking. It would surely send him into a rage. We went back to our HELLHOLE and I immediately went to check the children.

I felt an overwhelming need to hold them. I reached in the crib for my precious baby boy and cradled him as I laid us down next to my precious baby girl in her bed. I scooped her up in my other arm and held the children tightly, rocking us, ever so gently, back and forth. As I sucked in the strength of their youth and their soothing and calming scent, I began to mentally recap what had just happened.

I had to ask myself if it was all staged. Did he set it up to make his story more believable to me? He wanted me to think I needed his protection so I wouldn't leave. He sure didn't seem too worried someone might see us lurking around the back of the house. Almost as if he *knew* no one was going to come out and catch us. I didn't know what to believe anymore. I just knew it was very dangerous and someone was going to die if I didn't get us out of there. I just couldn't stand it one more day. I laid Christopher back in his crib and tucked them both in again.

We were all exhausted, including Chris. I lost count of how many days it had been since I last saw him sleep or eat something. He just kept shooting up and had lost so much weight he had become a skeletal image of himself. He had sold our living room set for drug money and started a new routine. He knew I wanted to leave him again and told me he couldn't live without me so he was going to kill himself and make me watch. He insisted I drove him to it. He would tie my wrists to the arms of a kitchen chair he brought into the living room so I could watch him try to overdose. He said he was sure any one of the next few fixes would kill him. I secretly wondered if the next one would put us all out of our misery. It was horrifying to have to sit there and witness this pathetic act of selfishness. It killed me to see how he let the drugs destroy him, us and our family. I couldn't watch it one more time. I was broken, he was broken. He had taken pieces of me and discarded them to diminish me to nothing but a sex slave. I had no more self-esteem, self- worth or confidence. We were both at the point of no return but I was in survival mode. I knew I had to get me and the children out of there. Maybe then he could get the professional help he so desperately needed.

While he was slouched down against the wall waiting to gain consciousness I prayed for the strength to stand up to him and just walk out. What was he going to do? Kill me? Well that was what he said he was going to do if I tried to leave again. If I went for the door I knew I would get a bullet in my back. He reminded me daily but it didn't matter anymore. I had thought and prayed about it so much, I felt I had to try again. I'd rather be dead than go through it one more day. My children deserved better, I deserved better and so did he. But he wasn't willing to sacrifice the drugs so we could be happy. I had to do what I had to do to get us out of there. If he killed me he would go to prison and my children would be safe with my family. I knew he was at his most vulnerable as soon as he regained consciousness. It only took a little while for him to be coherent again and steady on his feet so I had to make the best of the time he was still groggy. I felt an overwhelming surge of strength from within as I thought of my babies and anxiously waited for him to come to. This was it. I can't give up. If we don't get out, I will die trying!

After a short while Chris got up and stumbled over to untie me. He murmured, "We lucked out again. I see we made it through another one." I just wanted him to let go of me so I could check on the children and make my move while I was still feeling the surge of strength to stand up to him. I ran down the short hall to the children's room and found them content, playing with their toys. I grabbed Christopher's big diaper bag and started to throw in diapers and clothes for both of the children. I threw it over my shoulder along with my purse and swooped up Christopher in my left arm then grabbed Aprils' hand with my right hand. My heart was pounding in my chest, my hands shaking uncontrollably but my two angels were with me and I drew more strength from them. I remember April caressing the top of my hand she was holding as if to let me know it would be all right. My baby Christopher ever so lightly patted my back as he clung to my neck and wrapped his little legs around me as a baby chimp would cling to his mama. They were channeling their strength and energy to me and I sucked it in. I felt like a big volcano about to erupt as I barreled down the hallway to the front door. It was now or never.

Chris saw me heading for the door and yelled out, "Where do you think you're going?" He grabbed my arm. With all my might I yanked my arm from his grip and continued to the door. "What the FUCK do you think you're doing?" he yelled again. I looked back to see where he was and saw him shaking with rage looking for his gun in a panic. I reached down just enough to grab the doorknob with my left hand which was under Christopher's behind. Just then I heard a gunshot blast as I felt the swift wind of the bullet rush by my face. My attention shifted to the children to make sure neither of them had been hit by the bullet. They were shaken and crying but ok. No turning back, just keep moving forward, I told myself. Don't even look back again! I swung open the door to breathe the fresh air of freedom. It felt as though it was the first breath of my life!! I wanted to take it all in but there was no time to waste. The children and I were sobbing and shaking in fear as we heard more gunshots ring out behind us! We heard gunshot after gunshot which only made us run faster. Aprils' little legs couldn't keep up. I looked down at her as she looked up at me with her big beautiful blue eyes. I needed to hold her tight too so I lifted her up in my other arm and resumed my race. I didn't know where I was running, I just knew it had to be away from him and his evil hellhole.

The sounds of sirens and horns from emergency vehicles rang out in the close distance. Police cars screeched around the corners on both ends of the block. Oh my God!!! They were here for us already? Before we could get to the corner, the apartment and entire block was covered with police cars. An officer stopped and asked me if I was involved. I was tempted to say no so we could just keep going but he could tell all three of us were shedding tears and looked terrified. I couldn't lie to him. We needed his help and protection. I shook my head yes as I began to sob from the embarrassment and shame of it all. The officer directed us to his patrol car and told us everything would be okay. As we got in his car I begged him not to make us go back in the apartment because I could not bear it. I made him aware it had been about 3 months to the best of my recollection we had been held captive at gunpoint. He assured me he wasn't going to take us anywhere near the scene. We sat in the car with him for a while when another officer came over to tell him what was going on. Chris was in custody. He had shot out the television then shot around the apartment and the ceiling after the first shot at me. "That bullet must have went right between your heads, you're all very lucky," he said as he gave me a heartfelt nod and wink. He tapped his hand on the door and told his fellow officer to go ahead and take us home.

I held my babies tight as I wiped the streams of tears from their porcelain faces. Then I kissed the sweaty golden locks upon their heads, assured them we were safe and we would be at Grandmas' soon. I couldn't believe we were finally out of there. It all happened so fast I felt like it was a dream but it wasn't. We *were* out. Oh my God!! I will NEVER go back there again. Thank you God for letting us get out alive!

Then I thought, home, where is home for us? I mean, I know we're going to my parents' house and we will be safe there but it's not OUR home. I mentally gave myself a talking to...

I have to be strong for my babies. Their safety and well-being has to be my first priority and although it breaks my heart to admit it, being with their father was NOT what was best for them. I can't continue to put Chris first. I can't help him. He doesn't even think he *needs* help, which only makes matters worse. If our marriage is going to work it will be because he finally gave up the drugs and its dark, evil world and stopped being so selfish. I'm dreaming again. I see no sign of it happening any time soon. But we made promises to each other when we got married. Yeah, and I kept all of them while he continued to break each and every one of them. I tried so hard to please him but he didn't care how good of a wife and mother I tried to be. It's not about that with him. He told me he married me because I was a good girl, the kind he wanted for the mother of his children. He knew I would be long gone by the time he decided to give up the party life so he had to marry me while he had the chance. It was like Chris and I were always worlds apart. He was in the light and he kept me in the dark away from any other influence but his. It felt as though Chris was tucking me away our whole marriage. Like when you win a trophy of some kind and put it up on a shelf. You only take it out once in a while to admire it and stroke it a little then back on the shelf it goes protected from anything that could harm it. Who would have thought it would have needed protection from its protector? No one thinks they will ever need protection from the very person who shares their life and has taken marriage vows to love and protect them.

He was so caught up in his own world. He wanted to do his own thing and expected us to be there, years later, when he finally decided to grow up and take his responsibilities seriously. Well life doesn't just stand still while he's abandoning his responsibilities and his family. Time marches on, children grow up and I didn't want my children growing up like that. They deserved better and so did I. It seems I already wasted 4 years I will never get back. There was no cooperation from him and I couldn't save our marriage and our family on my own. I finally realized I was fighting a losing battle and had to give up hope on our marriage so I could put it to rest and move on. Everything was about to change. I was the only parent our children had to depend on. I had to make a home for the three of us now.

Chapter 9

MY PARENTS OF COURSE ACCEPTED US with open arms. I was so ashamed to have to go back again however I knew in my heart it was the last time. I needed to be strong for my children and myself and concentrate on getting a full-time job with benefits. I had to start building a new life for us without Chris. I didn't think I would ever see the old Chris again, not the man I married. Maybe a damaged version of himself if he quit right then and began to heal. I don't think anyone can do hard partying, boozing and heavy drug use for years and not suffer damage from it in some way.

I kept my husband in my prayers every night and hoped God would answer them. It was heartbreaking to realize I *had* to leave my husband in order to save our lives, all of our lives, including Chris'. It was very hard to do but every time I looked into my babies eyes, I knew I wanted to give them a better life which meant I had to want better for myself too. I had asked myself before if I loved him to the point of faulting my children but never answered. I knew then I could honestly say, yes, I was. I needed to start thinking differently and keep my focus there. Nothing or no one will ever be put before what is best for my children and me ever again.

I told my parents I was done with Chris and my dad gave me his attorneys' name and phone number. I was anxious to get the divorce started and decided to call first thing in the morning. I didn't know how long we would be with my parents, hopefully only a few months.

My dad went with me for the first visit to his attorney and I was assigned to one of his colleagues because his case load was too heavy. He led us to another office down the hall and introduced us to Mr. Donald Storm assuring us we were in good hands. Mr. Storm explained to us the divorce would cost only $500.00 if it was uncontested. We discussed all the pertinent details and he said he would get things started.

Little did I know it would create even more drama with Chris. He called my parents' house to tell me he had been bailed out of jail again by his friend who owned the family bar they all hung out at. I told him I started divorce proceedings and he would be contacted by my attorney. He told me it wasn't going to happen and I couldn't divorce him without his signature. He wasn't letting us go. He wasn't going to give up so easily. I had to appear strong and confident and replied, "Easily? We've been fighting for 4 years!" I told him I wasn't going to live like that anymore and the children and I deserved better. I reminded him those were his own words he spoke to me when I was still pregnant with our first child. I told him I had watched our lives go into a downhill spiral ever since due to his lack of responsibility, his immaturity, disrespect for me and his family and his out of control arrogant, selfish attitude. I also made it clear there was nothing he could say or do to change my mind, I was done and had to move on. I said goodbye and could hear him going on some rant as I lowered the receiver and hung up.

He kept harassing me with phone calls and coming to the house threatening to break the door down if I didn't go outside to talk with him but he didn't want to discuss the divorce. He would instead rant on about all the craziness. I could tell he was still on drugs even though he tried to hide it. He thought he was so slick trying to make me think he changed because he was showered, wearing clean clothes and reeking of his favorite cologne, Old Spice. He didn't even stop to think he was telling me the same old stories so how could I believe he was off the drugs? I really didn't know how much more of it I could handle but I knew of a way to end it temporarily so I asked if he heard from my attorney. Sure enough, it pissed him off and he fired up his Harley, the only thing it seemed he loved other than himself and off he went.

Things were calm for a few days then one morning after my parents left for work I heard the rumble of his motorcycle under the carport. Of course he waited until he knew I would be alone with the children. I opened the door to tell him to leave but he said he needed to talk to me about something. I assumed he was contacted by my attorney and was ready to discuss the divorce and visitations with the children so I went down the one step and walked over to him leaving the door barely ajar. As soon as Chris started running his mouth the door opened and April hopped down the step with baby Gitifer, as she called him, in tow. They began running around the motorcycle as I was once again listening to Chris ramble on about all the dangerous people who were out to get us. It literally made me sick to my stomach to see him and what he had let himself become, let alone listen to his evil stories again. At some point I had to not even entertain his stories anymore by simply listening to it. I had a little more strength to stand up to him then and realized I couldn't even be around him. Inside I was having an anxiety attack while trying not to show it to him. I was still so scared of him. I told him I didn't want to hear his stories anymore, picked Christopher up and set him on my hip. I went to grab Aprils' hand so we could go inside when Chris snatched her up, sat her in front of him on the gas tank and took off!

Scared out of my mind, I ran in the house with Christopher, slammed the door, and called 911! I told the dispatcher what happened. "He took my baby on the motorcycle, with no helmet, no protection! He's out of his mind on drugs! Please help me get my daughter back!" I cried in a panic. She said she would send a unit out to the house immediately.

It seemed like an hour, but the officers were there shortly. They asked for my story and where I thought he might go. "His grandparents live only a few blocks away," I told them. They sent a unit to Grandpa and Grandma McGaughey's house but he wasn't there. Then the officer asked me for a copy of our divorce decree. I told him it was in the process and we were not legally divorced yet. Much to my surprise he told me there was nothing they could do to help me get my daughter back. He explained if we were not legally divorced then Chris had every right to see his children. I said, "That's it? You can't help me? He took my three-year-old daughter on a motorcycle with no helmet and he is out of his mind on drugs!" The officer said, "I'm sorry, you'll have to try to get her back yourself!" I was dumbfounded! As the officers headed for the front door to leave I began to sob and closed the door behind them.

With tears streaming down my face I picked up Christopher and held him tight. I promised him I would get his sister back if it was the last thing I did. I felt so helpless though. I didn't know where to start. I was waiting for Chris to call me but he didn't. I prayed he would keep our daughter safe and would call soon. I tried to tell myself he would never hurt our children but I felt hesitant to believe it. After all, I never thought he would hurt me either. The man I married would never hurt me or the children but the reality was; he was no longer the same man.

Ok. Take a deep breath and think, I told myself. I had to wait for my mother to come home from work so she could watch Christopher and I could use her car to go looking for them. I was pacing the floor like a caged animal with a million different scenarios running through my head. I was trying to think of all his little hideouts but Lord knows I didn't know half of them. I waited for hours thinking and playing out every last horrible and gruesome scenario my mind could possibly imagine. I was terrified for my little girl. What if he has her with all those druggie meth heads he calls friends? The thought of any one of them even touching her made my skin crawl! I was getting angrier by the minute. How could he do this? He knew I would do whatever I had to, to get my baby girl back. He knew I would come to find him as long as he had one of our children. He always used our children as pawns against me to get his way.

Finally it was 3 o'clock in the afternoon and mom came home from work. We cried together as I told her what happened. Then the phone rang. Oh my God!! My heart about jumped out of my chest!

The Haunting Sliver of Light

It was Chris! He very pointedly stated, "If you ever want to see April again you need to go to the gas station on the corner of Maryland Parkway and Flamingo and wait at the payphone for me to call you." I felt like I was in a dream. Are you kidding me? And the cops couldn't HELP me? They had no idea how dangerous the situation was. My heart was racing and I started shaking uncontrollably, then he just hung up. I told my mom what he said. She handed me her car keys and said, "Go!" I gave my baby Christopher and mom a kiss goodbye and ran out the door as I thanked her.

All the way to the gas station I prayed he would have April with him so I can see with my own eyes she was okay. I parked the car and walked over to the payphone. My hands were still trembling as I was trying to light a cigarette to calm my nerves. All of a sudden I heard a car horn beep. I looked up and saw a taxicab creeping down the alley behind the gas station. Then I saw the back window roll down and Chris in the backseat waving for me to go over there. I quickly walked over to the taxi and peeked in to see if April was there with him. Thank God she was sitting right next to him safe and sound. She looked up at me with her angel face, smiled and said, "Hi mommy. Are you coming with us?" Before I could open my mouth Chris answered, "Yes she is. Come on mommy get in." I was very hesitant but then he took his 357 out of his waistband and pointed it in my face. I looked at the taxi driver who was watching in the rearview mirror. As our eyes met I gave him a scared, helpless look which I prayed he read the right way. His eyes were about to pop out of his head so I figured he saw the gun. I opened the door and sat next to Chris. He told the taxi driver to go to some dumpy motel on Koval Lane. I had to think fast and decide what to do and say in order to paint a clear enough picture for the taxi driver this was an ongoing and very dangerous situation. All the way to the motel I was talking to Chris about all the crazy things he was telling me, the people out to get me, the coffins they made for me and the children etc. so the taxi driver would understand I desperately needed his help.

I kept making eye contact with him in the rearview mirror to see if he was getting it. His eyes seemed to be glued wide open as he hung on our every word. He looked frightened yet very concerned. I could tell he caught on to what was happening. It was as if we were communicating telepathically. It wasn't the right time to make a move yet and he knew it. Wait…I'll let you know when, my eyes told him. When we pulled in front of the motel Chris made a serious mistake. He told the taxi driver to keep an eye on his two girls while he went in to get a room. As soon as he closed the taxi door the driver asked me if I wanted him to take off. I quickly responded, "Not yet! If you leave now, he will start shooting. Wait until he walks in the door then FLOOR IT!" I scooped April up in my arms as my eyes filled with tears. I could feel her little arms squeeze me with all her might. She had on a brave, beautiful smile but she was terrified too. All of a sudden the taxi driver took off. On the way back to moms' car, I told him I did not have any money and I just left my husband who is whacked out on drugs. I suggested if he could just follow me back to my moms' house I could get some money to pay for the fare from her. Visibly shaken, he touched the top of my hand resting on the back of the front seat and said, "Don't worry about it. Just get you and your daughter home safe," as he pulled up along the side of moms' car. I thanked him as April and I got out of the taxi then we jumped in the car and I drove home as quickly as I could.

Once we were in the house I locked the door behind me. As I was telling my mother what happened, I looked out the front window to the street. I said, "It's only a matter of time before he's back at the house and boy is he going to be pissed." No sooner did I get the words out of my mouth, there was Chris in another taxicab. I yelled to my mother, "Call the police! He's out there already!"

By this time my dad and brothers were home too. Everyone was scared and nervous because anytime Chris came to the house he was armed and it usually involved the police. My dad insisted I go out front to try and calm him down. I reluctantly made my way down the driveway to the sidewalk where the taxi was parked and Chris was getting out, leaving his door open. My heart was pounding as I was trying to anticipate what would happen next. I also didn't want to get too close to him in case he went to grab me. I figured if there was a little distance between us, I may have a chance to run into the house if he tried.

I was at the end of the driveway about to step onto the sidewalk when I told him my dad was on the phone with the cops and he needed to go before they got there but it only angered him and the situation escalated very quickly. He lunged at me as he could see I was intentionally keeping my distance. He grabbed hold of my arms and kept trying to push me into the cab as I tried to push back with my hands firmly against the car. I was begging with him to stop but he wouldn't listen. My mother and older brother, Kenny, were watching out the living room window, relaying everything to my dad so he could tell the dispatcher. Mom could see I was struggling to hold on and ran out to help while telling Kenny to make sure the kids didn't run outside. She went to pull Chris' arm off me which made him push her so hard her glasses flew off her face and she fell in the grass. Kenny ran out to help her and found her broken glasses. Chris grabbed me around the waist and tried again to throw me in the backseat of the taxicab. I tried to stretch my little body as far as I could. I reached out with the very tips of my toes to the back window and stretched my short little arms pass the open door to the passenger front window. I was holding on with all my might, pleading with Chris to stop. I looked inside and made eye contact with the cabdriver who was turned around watching everything but was in TOTAL SHOCK! A concerned and fearful look was upon his face as he tried to process what was going on. I kept yelling, "Please just go! Take off! Get out of here! He's trying to take me and the cops are on their way!" But he was frozen in disbelief. He just kept saying, "What's going on?" I turned my head and saw my dad come out of the house and start running down the driveway yelling, "The cops are on their way. Get out of here!" Just then, we began to see the police cars coming down the street. Chris grabbed me around the waist again only this time he pulled me off the car and tossed me aside with my family. He jumped in the cab and slammed the door. He wasn't about to go back to jail. In his usual arrogant fashion, he flipped me off as they sped away.

We were checking each other for injuries when the officers approached us. They asked if everyone was alright and if the "suspect" had gotten away in the taxicab. We assured them everyone was fine except moms' broken glasses. The officers motioned for us to go into the house so we all headed up the driveway. Once inside they took our statements and asked me for my divorce decree. When I told the officer it was in the process and Chris and I weren't legally divorced yet, he said there was nothing he could do and told us to call 911 if he returned. I was getting so tired of hearing that. So because we weren't legally divorced yet, he can treat me anyway he wants and put all our lives in danger? They had no idea how drugged up and dangerous Chris was all the time. They informed us there was nothing to press charges for since he didn't really hurt anyone or damage any property. The officers told us to have a good day as they left.

Chapter 10

MY PARENTS REALIZED THEY COULD NOT protect us and something needed to be done. The next morning I was told they made all the arrangements for Kenny to drive with me and the children to Chicago, our hometown. More specific, a suburb called, Melrose Park. My mom's brother, my Uncle Tony and Aunt Fran lived there with my cousin Georgette. They agreed to take us in so I could get a new start however there was no discussion with me. I wondered if my parents even considered me an adult the way they made all these plans without even consulting me but I knew in my heart it was what was best. I had to leave town to keep Chris from finding me and creating violent situations. I knew being at their house was putting them all in danger too and I would never forgive myself if something terrible happened to one of my family members. My dad gave me his Ford Mustang convertible and told me if I needed to sell it then so be it but until then it would get us there. Kenny was to fly back the day after we arrived. I was a little excited about going back home because I never wanted to move to Las Vegas to begin with. We were all very close before we moved to Las Vegas and as I reminisced, my minds' eye showed me a quick flashback of some of my favorite childhood memories.

A lot of them were spent at my Uncle Tony and Aunt Fran's house. I will never forget the beautiful Italian Feast every July. It seemed like miles of streets in Melrose Park were closed off for the Feast. The beginning was only 2 blocks from their house. You first came upon what seemed like endless amounts of food. For as far as you could see down the street there were vendors lined up selling Italian beef sandwiches, hot dogs, burgers, calzones, rolled pizza, Italian sausage on a stick, Italian ice, you name it. Beyond all the food was the best part of all for us kids, the huge carnival, with all the games and their prizes to be won and of course the rides. The Zipper was always my favorite and as I learned the very first time, you need to go on it with an empty stomach. The Feast went on every day for a whole week.

After a week of fun, games and feasting was the serious part, the whole reason for the feast. It was the procession of Our Lady of Mt. Carmel. People would carry a huge statue of The Blessed Mother holding the infant Jesus through the streets for hours as they walked, some even barefoot on the hot pavement, all around town and recited prayers aloud. I started to feel a little melancholy just thinking about it. I really missed everyone and thought it would be great to reconnect with the whole family including 2nd and 3rd Aunts, Uncles and cousins.

Aunt Fran and Uncle Tony lived upstairs from her mother, Virginia. It was actually Virginia's house, the same house Aunt Fran grew up in with her 2 brothers. Virginia was 100% Italian about 4'10" and such a loving woman. To the best of my memory she was always smiling too. She made endless pots of meatballs and Italian sausage in homemade gravy, as REAL Italians call it, the old timers would say. There was a sprawling trellis across the yard embodied with grapevines which yielded an overabundance of plump, juicy, delicious concord grapes. The patio table and chairs were strategically placed under it and was always set and ready to feed family, friends, neighbors and strangers alike. I remember sitting there with my brothers and cousins waiting to go to the carnival while we munched on the lupini beans in the bowls on the table.

WE HAD A QUICK BREAKFAST, PACKED our bags and loaded up the car in hopes we would be long gone when Chris got his next urge to surge. Kenny informed me, "The plan is to drive straight through with us taking turns driving so we could get sleep without stopping. No stopping except to use the restroom." I remember thinking he was just like our father in that aspect. Every summer for probably 7 or 8 years we went to Las Vegas on vacation. My dad insisted on driving straight through with no stops except for the restroom. It would give us more time for fun once we got there, he always told us. This meant two days straight in the car. Oh boy. I hoped the children wouldn't get too restless and Christopher wouldn't get a diaper rash. I made a mental note to make sure I checked him every time we stopped. We said our good-byes and took off.

First stop was to gas up. While Kenny was pumping gas I ran in the store to buy some drinks and snacks for the road and threw in some No Doze. I was going to need it. We had a cooler with sandwiches and fruit too so there was no need to even stop to eat. As we drove for hours on end I began to wonder when Kenny was going to ask me to drive but the truth is, I secretly wished I wouldn't have to. I was so nervous and feeling like Chris was following us even though I knew he most likely wasn't. I couldn't help it though. He always showed up at the most inopportune times. The only transportation he had was the motorcycle and I didn't hear it or see him anywhere thank God. Believe me I was looking all around the whole time.

I saw it was a little past dinner time so I reached into the cooler for some sandwiches and passed them out. The next few hours seemed to fly by. I started to think I should probably call Patti the next time we get a pee break. I knew she would be worried and now I wouldn't be in town for what I thought was going to be a long time. It wasn't too much longer before Kenny pulled off the road into a rest stop. We all had to use the restroom and I reminded myself I needed to change Christopher.

I let the kids run around on the grass for a bit while Kenny carefully examined the map. It was dark, probably around 10pm. It was my turn to drive so he wanted to make sure he was giving me correct instructions before he went off to sleep. I told him I hadn't used the bathroom yet so I could run back to pop a couple No Doze and call Patti really quick. I peed, popped the pills and ducked around the corner where I saw a pay phone earlier. When Patti answered the phone I told her not to talk just listen and grab a pen and paper. I told her I didn't have much time and quickly explained what was going on and where we were going. She wrote down my Aunt and Uncles' phone number and address on a small pad of paper by the telephone. I told her when we were expecting to arrive there and said I would be in touch soon. We said our goodbyes and I hung up the phone quietly as I got goose bumps looking out into the creepy darkness. I felt like someone was watching me through the trees and I hoped it wasn't Chris. I suddenly thought what if he IS following us? Of course it was just my nerves because of all the times he had shown up out the blue. I got a chill and ran back to the car. After Kenny's direction discussion I carefully secured Christopher in his car seat and April in her seat belt and took the drivers' seat. Boy was I on edge. I kept looking in the rear view mirror expecting to spot him behind us. I told myself to take some deep breaths, settle in and calmed down. I was to drive through the night while everyone else slept. Not wanting to wake anyone I kept the music on very low so I had a little something for company and wouldn't get distracted with my nervous thoughts. I remember hoping we were leaving all the sinister stuff behind us as I glanced in the rearview mirror as if to see it staring back at me.

As the sun began to wake, it filled the sky with warm beautiful colors. It was quite the contrary to the eerie darkness of the night sky just hours before and Kenny woke as the rising sun warmed his face. I said, "good morning" as he sat up from his slumped position and began to stretch. After looking around for a bit he said he wasn't sure where we were so he suggested I pull over at the next rest stop. He said he had to pee and wanted to get his map out. Our conversation woke the children from their slumber and they told me they were hungry. We came upon the next rest stop pretty quick so I pulled off the freeway and into a parking spot right in front of the restrooms. It felt so good to get out and stretch. I got the children out and we all headed for the restroom.

When we met Kenny back at the car he was putting away his map. He was pleased we were making good time and told me we should be to Melrose Park by nightfall. I was so happy to hear it because I hated being cooped up in a car for hours on end. I have restless leg syndrome and it acts up every time I'm on a road trip. We had some fruit for breakfast and let the children run around for a while. Then with everyone buckled up, we were on the road again. I tried to lay my head down and get some sleep but the children were full of energy and raring to go after a full nights' sleep. They were teasing each other and reaching for each other to play. I watched them giggle as my heart filled with thankfulness and joy while my eyes welled up with tears. In my thoughts, I thanked God for my babies and for letting us still be alive and have a chance for a better life.

The last part of the trip seemed the longest because we were all very anxious to get there but we managed to keep the kids busy singing songs and with guessing games. All the way to Chicago Kenny never asked me anything about what was happening between me and Chris. I got the feeling he just wanted to stay out of it and I was content with it because the less he knew the better off he was.

We were all thrilled to finally arrive at Uncle Tony and Aunt Fran's house. Just stepping out of the car we could smell the aroma of Aunt Fran's homemade gravy. I was sure she had a pot of meatballs and sausage on the stove. Thank goodness because we were all very hungry and tired of sandwiches and fruit.

It wasn't the best of circumstances but we were all glad to see each other. Once upstairs with our luggage I felt it was ok to relax knowing we were far away from Chris. There was no way he could find us. He had never even met my Chicago family and he didn't have anyone's phone numbers or addresses either. We had a beautiful meal and visit with our favorite Aunt, Uncle and cousin. Uncle Tony opened the sofa bed for me and the children and Kenny was to sleep in the little spare bedroom on the bottom bunk. I tucked the children in and we all turned in for the night.

The next morning Uncle Tony took Kenny to the airport on his way to work. I think my brother was a little anxious to get back to work and school. Maybe a little relieved too. His part was done. He got us there safe and sound and he was ready to get home and resume his own life. I couldn't blame him although I was very thankful he took time off to help me and the children get there.

I made breakfast for the kids then started looking through the newspaper for a job while they watched cartoons. By the time Aunt Fran and Uncle Tony got home from work I had a long list of potential employers I had started to check out. Aunt Fran suggested the Hispanic woman across the street to babysit the children while I worked so I went over to talk to her. She had children around the same ages of mine they could play with which was a plus but it was next to impossible to communicate with her because she didn't speak English. Not one word, her children were interpreting for her. I really had no other choice so I had her watch the children a few times while I was on job interviews but when I picked them up everyone was frustrated. Oh, no. I can't have someone watching my children who can't even communicate with them. They were going through enough and I thought it would only hinder them more. I wasn't at all comfortable with it so I decided against it.

About 5 or 6 weeks went by and I was still unemployed. I was beginning to get discouraged when my cousin Mary Ellen called me and told me she got me an interview with someone she knew. She worked for the State of Illinois in personnel. I had to go to downtown Chicago for the interview and had no idea where I was going. When we moved to Las Vegas I was only 17 years old and just began to drive the year before. I never even drove on the freeways and expressways in Chicago much less downtown traffic. I was so scared I was going to get lost but Mary Ellen gave me good directions. She even met me at the front door in the lobby when I arrived at the office building. She directed me into a small office to take a typing test then she took me to the interviewer. It seemed to go well but I didn't know anything when I left. Mary Ellen said they would be in touch.

On the drive home I was beginning to feel a bit defeated wondering why it seemed no one wanted to hire me. I was being completely honest with each potential employer about my situation. Then it hit me. Maybe my honesty was exactly what was keeping me from being employed. I mean, I was telling them I was in the middle of a divorce back in Las Vegas and they probably figured I would be taking time off to go back for court not to mention the possibility of me deciding to move back. I would discuss it with Uncle Tony and Aunt Fran over dinner.

I WAS HELPING AUNT FRAN CLEAR the table after dinner when the phone rang. Georgette answered it in her room and the next thing I knew she was calling me. She said the phone was for me and when I asked her who it was she said, "They didn't say, just asked for you." I asked her if it was a woman or a man, holding my breath waiting for her answer. "It's a girl," she said. So I went to her room to talk thinking it was Patti. She was the only person outside of my family who knew where I was. I took the phone and said "Hello?" Much to my surprise, Chris said, "Hello Karen, I found you!!!"

I instantly got the chills and goose bumps sprung up all over my body as I processed the sound of his voice. I was dumbfounded. I immediately took a step out of the room and made eye contact with Aunt Fran motioning for her to pick up the kitchen phone to listen in. "How did you find me here?" I asked. He responded with "Karen, it was a sign from God!" "What are you talking about?" I asked as I returned to the bedroom and sat down on the bed. He explained he went over to Patti's house to talk to her and see if she had any idea where I was because he was so worried. He told her it was like the kids and I just fell off the face of the earth. He had been spying at everyone's houses he could think of and there was no sign of us anywhere. He told her he believed his worst fear had come true. The children and I were kidnapped and sold into white slavery or killed.

Up until then Patti had no idea of the bizarre stories Chris had cooked up in his drug crazed head. He said she got very nervous and said she had to use the restroom. He continued, "It was then, while I was waiting for her to come back I looked down at the empty pad of paper sitting on the table. The sun was shining on it just right so I could see the imprint of something written on the page before. So I found a pencil by the phone, started to scribble across the page and was amazed at what appeared. It was your Aunt and Uncle's address and phone number. I took the scribbled page with the information and shoved it in my pocket then yelled to Patti to let her know I was leaving. I figured Patti was the only friend you told where you were going so I would just have a chick ask for you. Once I heard your voice and verified you were there I could make arrangements." To which I replied, "Arrangements for what?" "Well to come and get you and the kids of course," he replied. Immediately we heard my Aunt Fran's voice say sternly and clear, "Now you listen to me. If you so much as step one foot on Chicago soil no one will ever hear from Chris Roberts again. Do you understand me?" I was holding my breath as I anticipated he would reply with his usual arrogant, cockiness. No one told *him* what to do, especially a woman. But there was only complete silence as he processed what he was just told. Then we heard a "click." He just hung up. I exhaled a big sigh of relief as my trembling hand hung up the phone. Chris had never met my Chicago family and it was clear he was intimidated.

Chapter 11

WITHIN A COUPLE OF DAYS I received a call from my attorney. Contrary to his presumptions, the court wanted me to be present for the divorce hearing so I had to go back to Las Vegas. Chris had called also after getting his notice to appear. He made sure to call in the morning assuming Aunt Fran and Uncle Tony were at work and told me he knew I had to come back for the divorce. He was so pleased, as if he was the victor of the small quest. He insisted on knowing the date and picking us up at the airport for a brief visit. I told him I didn't think it was a good idea and I already had a ride but he was persistent. As he started rambling to his defense I began to feel guilty. It had been months since the children had time with their father. I looked at my babies and my heart began to soften. It's a short drive to my parents' house from the airport, I thought, so I gave in and told him I would let him know the flight information when I received it.

My mom was not thrilled when I told her Chris was picking us up. She was anxious to see us and put her torment to rest. Chris had been calling her before he found us telling her of his coffin and white slavery theories. I reassured her he was bringing us right to her house. My parents had made the flight arrangements and gave me the information. They also told me I would be staying in Vegas since I hadn't found a job yet. There was no sense in going back and forth. I felt as though they were making all these decisions for me but since they were paying for the airfare I really didn't have a choice. I informed Uncle Tony and Aunt Fran of the plans but of course they already knew of them since they had discussed it with my parents. The children and I were to leave the next day as there was no reason to stay any longer.

The next morning I was packing again. I thanked Uncle Tony and Aunt Fran and we said our goodbyes. Uncle Tony took us to the airport and wished us well. The plan was for mom and Kenny to drive there and pick up the car at a later date.

I THOUGHT I WAS PREPARED TO see Chris again however the minute I laid eyes on him I was sure I was wrong. He still looked terrible, a skeletal version of the man I married. I hoped he had quit using drugs when I left and was on the road to recovery but it was clearly not the case. As soon as the hugs were over he was rushing us to the baggage pickup. I asked what he was in such a hurry about and he said so we could run out before anyone would see us. It was obvious his paranoia was still very real in his mind. I was glad we were around other people and thought I would just call my mom from a pay phone to pick us up but he wasn't about to let it happen. After we picked up the luggage he said he had a taxi waiting out front which he hurried us into. He told the driver to go to a motel just down Paradise Rd. from the airport. He already had a room there and said he just wanted to visit with us for a while. Once again I felt as though I had no choice. Then I felt bad and thought it would do the children good to have a visit with their father. Maybe with just us in the motel room with no druggie buddies or interruptions we could have some quality time together as a family. Then I thought maybe he planned it that way. He knew all I wanted was for us to be a family and thought he would give me a taste of it to lure me to go back. It was the same old thing it seemed but since we had been away for months I decided to keep an open mind and once again give him the benefit of the doubt.

We followed him up to the second floor room. When he opened the door I saw it had two beds and immediately knew he planned on us spending the night. Oh Lord, not again. Please!! I reluctantly stepped inside the room guiding the children with me. I sat my purse down on the small table by the door and turned toward him as he turned toward me, setting down the suitcases. Our eyes met and I'm sure he saw the uncertainty in mine, I couldn't hide it. He immediately began to tell me he needed to spend one more night with us and if I still wanted to go in the morning he would let us leave. "I promise," he said holding up his hand as if he was swearing on a Bible. The problem was his promises meant nothing to me anymore. He had broken every one he had ever made to me. I began to worry if we would make it through the night. I was getting very scared again wondering if it was all a plan to commit a family murder and suicide. I didn't know anymore what kind of things he was cooking up in his drug-filled head. I started to open the door and began to tell him I changed my mind. It wasn't a good idea after all and the children and I were going to leave but he firmly pushed the door closed. He said harshly with his arm extended over my head, "One more night, Karen." I conceded and shook my head yes. I thought at least if things go awry and I screamed for help, someone would hear me. The motel was surely full with people.

I saw he still had his 357 sidekick as he removed it from his waistband and laid it on the nightstand next to the bed closest to the door. I didn't want to rock the boat and it was getting late so I decided to give the children a bath and get them ready for bed. After I washed them I let them play in the tub for a bit to pass some time but then he asked me what was taking so long. I tried to stall telling him they were so good on the plane I was giving them a little extra play time but he decided it didn't matter. He wanted me to get done with the bath so they could go to bed, so much for spending some quality time together as a family. I took a deep breath, pulled the plug and stood Christopher up as I wrapped a towel around him. "Come on sweetie," I said to April. She stood up and took her towel from me. They jumped on the bed in the corner as I dried them off. While the jammies were going on they were both yawning and getting sleepy eyed. I tucked them in and they were out in a few minutes.

I had decided to go to sleep after I got the kids in bed so there was no drama but when I was in the bathroom brushing my teeth I heard some strange noises. I came out to find Chris had taken one of the sliding doors off the closet. I asked him what he was doing as I went to sit on the bed. He quickly grabbed my arm and flung me to the floor. "What the hell are you doing Karen? I thought I taught you better than that. Those motherfuckers are probably right downstairs under us. All they have to do is take a big long sword and thrust it through the ceiling right into us in bed and we're dead! That's why I have to slide this door in between the mattress and box spring," he explained as he proceeded to do it.

Once again I was at a loss for words. It was quite clear he was still deep into the drugs. Just get in bed and go to sleep I told myself, but he wasn't going to let me sleep. He kept me up half the night with his same horror stories then he finally came down from his high. He finally crashed and I was able to get a few hours of sleep. I was surprised but very happy he didn't initiate sexual contact. I was so turned off by him by then and I knew he would just force me to accommodate.

As soon as I opened my eyes in the morning, I was trying to figure out who I could call to pick us up. We were kind of close to my parents' house and I wouldn't mind walking but I had the children and the suitcases. I had to think of someone who didn't work and Caroline came to mind. She was one of Chris' friend's sisters who I had become friends with. She lived practically around the corner and she didn't work. I called her and she said, "Sure, I'll be there in a few." Thank God. I told Chris she was coming to give me and the children a ride to my parents' house and she would be there shortly. I got us all dressed so we were all ready to go as soon as Caroline got there. I looked outside to see her pulling up already. What a relief. I quickly took the children down to her and put them in the car. As we hugged I whispered to her, "I'm so afraid of Chris and he is losing his mind" then turned around certain he was watching me. When I went back up to the room to get the luggage I found him on the floor in the corner of the closet in the fetal position covering his face with his hands and sobbing. A part of me wanted to console him but I knew I had to go while I had the chance. So I said goodbye and left.

For a while I was on edge and afraid he would come back and try to take me or the children because his threatening phone calls resumed. He used our children as pawns to get what he wanted from me and knew I would come to him if he had them. Once I was home from job hunting I wouldn't leave the children or the house. I was hopeful I would hear from one of the many financial institutions I applied at since my work experience was in banking.

Then one evening I decided to call Patti to finally let her know we were back in Las Vegas and catch her up on things. I dialed her phone number wondering where on earth to begin. The phone rang only twice and she picked up. "Hello?" she cautiously inquired. I answered, "Hi Patti, its Karen." Before I could go on she asked, "Are you and the babies o.k.?" with a quiver in her voice. "Yes, that's why I'm calling. To tell you we are back in Las Vegas and staying with my parents again." I explained what had been going on and how I was afraid to leave the children. She decided we needed to get together and catch up. "What are you doing Friday night?" she asked suggesting I needed a break from it all to unwind and relax for a while. It was only Wednesday so I told her I would think about it and check with my mom about watching the children but deep down I knew I had every intention of calling her back only to tell her a fib......my mom said no.

I was still so nervous about leaving the children but getting together with Patti seemed to be all I had on my mind for a day and half. I was so torn about a simple decision to go over to a friends' house for the evening. Was it silly? I asked myself. It's only a few hours. Everyone at the house, besides me was feeling more relaxed since there hadn't been any dangerous situations with Chris, just the phone calls but I knew him too well. I knew it was only a matter of time. My gut was still telling me not to leave the house.

Friday evening mom and I were talking as we cleaned up after dinner and I mentioned what Patti suggested. She agreed with her. She told me to go and assured me the children would be ok. I was a little surprised but it made me entertain the idea even more. I couldn't remember the last time I got to enjoy a visit with a friend. It would be a breath of fresh air, although my emotions were still in a little bit of a tug of war over what I should do. Reluctantly, I decided to go. I called Patti and told her I would head over to her place after I got the children to sleep. She was so happy to hear it. After their bath I tucked my babies into bed then talked with mom for a minute or two. I think she sensed I was stalling because she went to get her car keys, handed them to me and said, "Go, have a good time. Everything will be fine."

I shook my head affirmatively and took a deep breath as I reached for the keys she was holding out. With her reassurance I began to get a little excited to take a break from the stress and tension of always having to be on guard. I told myself it was just a break while someone else was on watch. I would be back in a few hours, way before the children would wake up. I just never knew when Chris would strike again and it's what made me so anxious. Now if I could just relax a little it would be great.

I tiptoed into the back bedroom where my angels were lying in their heavenly slumber. Ever so gently I touched my lips to each of their satin soft cheeks and planted a "protective kiss" from mommy. "Please Lord, keep my babies *and* my family safe for the night while I'm away," I silently prayed as I backward tiptoed out of the room and quietly closed the bedroom door. I said thank you and goodbye to mom on my way out the door.

Heading down the street I realized I was almost out of cigarettes so I decided to stop at the 7-11 down the street on Maryland Pkwy. I walked in and got a big gulp then went up to the cashier and asked for a pack of Virginia Slim Menthol Lights. I paid the cashier and walked out to the car. Just as I was putting the key in the door Chris came up behind me. He shoved his trusty ole friend 357 into my ribs and told me to get in. Once

I was in the driver's seat he hit the lever to push the seat back and sat right on my lap. "What are you doing Chris?" I asked. He told me to shut up and drove us down Maryland Pkwy to Russell Rd. where there was a dirt lot outside the airport runway where people went to watch the planes land and take off. He didn't say much only that he was going to have to teach me a lesson. For what now, I thought. Fear immediately overcame me. I knew all too well what he meant. After he turned off Russell Rd. onto the dirt lot he drove down quite a ways in order to not be around any other cars. And just my luck it wasn't packed that night and my chances of someone seeing I was being held against my will were looking pretty dismal. My heart was pounding and I noticed we were the only car at the far end of the runway. It's so loud with all the airplanes no one would even hear me if I screamed. After he parked, he turned the car off and slid over to the passenger side. I looked over at him as I trembled with anticipation of what he was going to do to me. Driving in, it looked like he was alone in the car. Surely no one could see me underneath him in the driver's seat. Was I going to die here? Why did I give in? This is exactly why I didn't want to leave the house. I should have listened to my gut and my instincts. I knew him better than anyone else. I knew he was just lying and waiting it out until he saw me alone out in public. He always told me he did his best work at night under the cover of darkness. What was I thinking? It had only been a short time, he wasn't done and he wasn't going to stop.

He noticed I was looking at the metal bar he had, so decided to explain it was the handicapped bar he broke off the wall in a hotel bathroom. When I asked him what for, he said he was using it for a walking stick and protection when he was on the streets. Then he told me if I didn't cooperate he would show me what else it was good for. He began to stroke my hair and tell me how much he loved and missed me and wanted us to be together as a family again. He said he wanted to make love and started to take my shirt off. I grabbed his hand to stop him. I told him no and it infuriated him. He became full of rage and started screaming at me about all the dangerous things he said were happening and said it was next to impossible to protect us if we weren't with him. Funny, when he's not around everything is calm. No one is stalking me or trying to take me. Only him! He vowed he wasn't going to let me go again then suddenly his mood changed and he broke down and began to sob. His head fell onto my chest. I knew these sudden mood changes from extremely agitated to deep sadness only meant one thing. He was coming down from his high.

He was living with his grandparents and brother, Chuck, again and decided to take me there. It was getting late but I was hoping someone would be awake when we got there so I would have some help with getting away. He had me drive to the house and park. We got out of the car and he directed me up the driveway, through the little gate he opened for me. We started up the walkway when he stopped short, right in front of his bedroom window. He told me we were going to crawl in through the window so no one in the house would know I was there otherwise they would call the police. Even his grandparents and brother were afraid of him at this point. He had threatened to kill every one of them too if they got in his way. He opened the window and lifted me up so I could get in then he followed. Once we were in the house, I tried to make a little noise to alert someone but Grandma and Grandpa McGaughey were elderly and couldn't hear a damn thing once they took their hearing aids out. I figured my best bet was for Chuck to hear us. His bedroom was right next to Chris' but my plan didn't work because he wasn't home. Chris had hurried me in the window so quickly when we got there I didn't notice Chucks' car wasn't in the garage.

A million things were running through my head again. Did Patti call my house and tell my mom I never made it there? Were the police out looking for me? And if so, why wouldn't they check his grandparents' house? Everyone is probably wondering if I'm dead!!! We were lying on the bed fully clothed as I anticipated him initiating sex again. But he didn't. He just held me from behind. I wanted to face the door just in case someone opened it. They would know immediately by the look on my face, I was not there by choice and needed their help. He just whispered quietly in my ear. He said he received a call from our landlord of the apartment to inform Chris he was suing us. I asked him why and he said when I left he had chopped up our king size waterbed with his machete and flooded the apartment. Then he told me a process server came to his grandparent's house with the divorce papers and when the guy went to hand him the papers he said he moved his hand and just let the wind take them away. The pressure was building for both of us. I could feel his chest jerking as he sobbed trying to hold it in. He begged me not to go through with the divorce and to bring our family back together. He said he wasn't going to sign the divorce papers and reiterated I wouldn't be able to divorce him if he didn't sign. He also made it clear he wouldn't be showing up in court believing his absence would delay the proceedings. The court date was only a few days away and what he didn't know was I had already anticipated him not signing the papers so I put an ad in the newspaper following my attorneys' advice. It only had to run for 6 weeks with no response in order for a non-contested victory and his time was up.

Trying to keep him calm I caressed his arms in front of me and began reminiscing of happier times when we first met and we both fell asleep. When we woke in the morning, he had a change of heart and told me he was going to let me go home. We walked out to the living room where his grandparents were sitting watching television. They got up very early and were already done with breakfast. They were surprised as hell to see me there. I said hello to them, we exchanged hugs and I made my way to the front door. As I thought, they knew immediately by the look on my face, he held me there against my will all night. I was holding my breath all the way secretly praying he wasn't going to flip out as I walked out the door. Once through the threshold I practically ran to the car, got in, slammed the door and locked it. Thank God! I hurried home.

Chapter 12

Mom greeted me with, "Oh thank God you're alright! What happened? Where were you all night?" Her words rang throughout the house and within seconds the whole family was surrounding me anxiously awaiting my answers. I told them what happened and let them know Chris did not hurt me he just wouldn't let me go until the morning. There was an astounding sigh of relief, all in unison. "You better call Patti. She's been worrying all night too," mom ordered. Apparently they had called each other a couple of times before turning in for the night.

My hands were still shaking as I dialed Patti's number. It rang one time and she pounced on it! It seemed as though she was sitting right in front of the phone just waiting for it to ring. "Hello?" she said with a frightened yet intrigued tone. "I'm so sorry you had to worry so much last night," I started with. "What happened to you? It was Chris again right?" She demanded answers. I knew she wasn't mad at me it was the situation everyone was upset about. We all hoped the night before would be the end of all the havoc but I knew in my heart Chris was not done. In his head he believed he was only trying to protect us from the scum he brought into our lives but there was no one else following me but HIM!!! As far as he was concerned, this is exactly why I needed his protection. Because I didn't see the people following me, he insisted. He refused to see his drug addiction was most of our problems.

Surprisingly, we had an incident-free rest of the day and night but I couldn't let my guard down again. Like I said, it was only a matter of time. How much was the question. How long next time would he lay low pounding meth into his veins while he conjured up all kinds of schemes to try and force me to come back to him again? It had been a nice peaceful weekend but I was on edge waiting for the ball to drop.

FINALLY MY COURT DATE HAD ARRIVED. It had been almost a year since I escaped from the apartment and started divorce proceedings. When I arrived at the law firm, Mr. Storm peeked out of his office and we made eye contact. He waved me into his office and closed the door behind me. I could tell he had something he wanted to discuss and assumed he was going to brief me about what to expect in court. Instead he handed me some papers and began to explain there were extra charges because of all the times Chris had called him with questions and to harass and threaten him. He wanted me to sign a contract stating I would pay the extra amount. I tried to process it all quickly to determine what to do. I didn't feel I should pay him any more money. After all, it *still is* a non-contested divorce but he made it clear we wouldn't be heading to the court room if I didn't sign it. I wasn't about to argue with him 15 minutes before my court time. I wanted the divorce NOW! I had waited so long already. I decided I would take care of the issue later and just signed the papers. He tucked them into my file which he tossed into his briefcase and we headed down the street to the courthouse. I was only asked a few questions on the stand and as I figured, Chris was not present. Thank goodness. My attorney also explained to the judge, he himself witnessed how deranged Chris was and he insisted it was too dangerous for the children to be around him unsupervised. I was granted my divorce and sole custody of the children with only supervised visitations for Chris because of his drug abuse.

I was so happy thinking everything was behind us but it was far from over. A few days later Chris called me on the phone boasting again he would never sign the divorce papers making it impossible for me to divorce him. Again he repeated the divorce could not happen without his signature. I let him ramble on and get it all out then I informed him we were already divorced and he was furious. He accused my attorney of being shady and pulling strings to make the divorce happen even though he had not agreed to it. I explained to him I didn't need his approval to divorce him and assured him everything was done legally and by the book. He was beside himself as he saw he was no longer in control and just hung up. I, on the other hand, started to feel empowered knowing I was back in control of my own life. I would no longer have to listen to the police tell me there was nothing they could do because we weren't legally divorced. I was then confident if Chris tried anything again the charges would stick. No more loopholes allowing his friends to bail him out within 24 hours so he could come right back and wreak more havoc. I was so relieved to finally have the divorce complete. It was a long time coming and I decided to go ahead with my thoughts of having a divorce party to cement the occasion in my life.

The plans were made for Kenny, Mom and my younger brother, Kevin, to drive to Chicago to pick up the Mustang and Dad was going on a golfing trip to California with some friends while they were gone. Perfect! It was a couple of weeks away so I had time to make my plans for the party. When I called Juliana to tell her I was divorced and arranging a party she was so excited to have another reason to go to Las Vegas and quickly booked a flight. I made arrangements for the children to spend the night with their part time babysitter, Debbie, who lived across the street from Aunt Rita and Uncle Ronny.

There was no contact from Chris for close to a week and I began to think maybe he finally got it through his head we were done and he would leave me alone. I wanted him to be a good father to our children but there was nothing left inside me for him. I hoped he would quit doing the drugs and get his life in order so he could be there for our children. I had every intention of giving him more than the supervised visitations he was awarded in court as long as he showed me he was off the drugs. I kept him in my prayers and pleaded with God to help him see what he needed to do to have a better life and a chance at happiness before he killed himself with the drugs.

The house was quiet. Everyone was sound asleep. I had just finished watching a movie, brushed my teeth and went to bed. I started to fade off to sleep in the middle of my prayers when I was startled by the ringing of the phone. It was after midnight so I instantly knew it was Chris. I quickly snatched the receiver up to answer hoping it didn't wake anyone else.

He was high, angry and started threatening me again. He said, "I'm going to ask you one question and you better think wisely before you answer because your life depends on it. Are you telling me there is no chance of you coming back to me?" I tried to calm him down by telling him it was late and if he would just wait until morning I would bring the children over to his grandparents' house so we could all visit and we could talk then but I guess it was the wrong answer. It infuriated him and he responded with this rant,

"I'm coming over there right now and I'm going to kill the kids right in front of your face so you know how it feels to be without them and then I'm going to kill you in front of your whole fucking family. By that time, everything I lived for will be gone and splattered in blood all over your fucking fathers' house. Then I'll shoot myself so we can be together for eternity!"

I didn't even have time to respond. He just slammed the phone down. I immediately called 911 and told the dispatcher what he said. She asked if he was at the house yet and I said with a panic in my voice, "No but he only lives a couple blocks from me. He will be here any minute. Please send officers, he always has his gun!" I was dumbfounded by her response. She told me she couldn't send a unit out just yet and I would have to call her back when he got to the house and only if he was causing a disturbance. I slammed the receiver down as I grumbled, "Oh my God!" All I could think about was him saying he was going to kill my babies first so I instinctively ran into their room and scooped Christopher up in my arms running down the hall, through the family room and down the other hallway to my parents' room. They woke as they heard me telling myself everything was going to be ok. But it wasn't. I handed the baby to my mother and told my dad to call 911 because Chris was on his way over and quickly explained what Chris' plan was then I ran back to get April. Just as I got back in their room to plop April on the bed we heard the rumble of Chris' motorcycle pulling up under the carport.

I ran on my tiptoes back to the front of the house so I could peek out the window to see where he was when I heard a tapping sound coming from the children's room. I ran to see what it was and found him gently tapping the handle of his 357 on the window as if he was trying to wake the children and get their attention. After no response he hit the bottom corner of the window hard with the gun breaking a softball size hole in it. I backed out of the room stopping at the doorway and continued to watch the window, peeking around the corner. I saw his fingers come through the hole and move the curtain over to look in at the children. Seeing an empty bed fueled his rage. I heard him talking to himself, cussing me out for having moved the children already as he walked across the front yard making his way to the front door. I moved down the hallway to follow him and was startled as he began to bang on the door. He tried to kick the door in but without success. I tried to calm him by talking to him through the door. I told him my dad was on the phone with the police and telling them everything that was happening. I tried to get him to leave before the police got there but he wasn't having it. There was a short pause in his ranting and banging so I ran down the hall to my parents room to ask if the police were indeed on their way. The adrenaline was mounting and I wanted the police to stop him before he got in and possibly hurt someone. My dad was still on the phone with the dispatcher when I heard Chris in the back yard ranting again. My dad told me to go out there and try to reason with him but I wasn't about to step foot out of the house and right into his fury. I slightly pulled the curtain away from the edge of the sliding glass door and peeked out to see where he was and what he was doing. To my utter amazement he was picking up one of the picnic table benches and raised it over his head. I suddenly had a huge lump in my throat instinctively knowing he was about to throw it through the sliding glass door. I simultaneously thought I was so glad I didn't open the curtains while I ran back away from the door just as the bench went flying through the glass. There was a huge crash! When I looked back Chris and I made eye contact. I saw what resembled a demon stepping through a black hole into our world, his eyes on fire with rage as he pointed his 357 at me! It was terrifying! I instinctively ran back down the hall to my parents room and could hear the glass crunching beneath his feet as he began chasing me yelling, "Karen, I'm going to shoot if you don't stop!" At the same time I heard dad tell the dispatcher she might as well just send the coroner with 8 body bags because he was now in the house threatening to shoot! I was petrified I would feel a bullet enter my body at any second but I just couldn't stop running. I entered my parents room, rounded the corner and glanced over toward the intense piercing shrills of everyone screaming. My dad slammed down the receiver, jumped on the bed to hold onto mom and my babies while my grandmother and brothers were huddled together in front of them. Even the 2 dogs joined the choir, all while Chris ranted close behind me. I ran until I couldn't go any farther and found myself in the shower with him finally making contact.

I impulsively began to cry as I crunched down in the fetal position gently bringing him with me. I tenderly held his arms around me as if to comfort a crying infant and whispered to him, "I don't believe you really want to hurt any of us. You're a good person Chris but all this dangerous stuff has to stop before someone gets hurt or killed and you end up in prison. I don't want that for you. Please, you have to quit the drugs. They have turned you into something evil and I'm terrified of you!" He turned me around to hold me proper and sunk into me laying his head on my chest and began to sob. I felt my heart thumping at a rate I'm sure it had never reached before praying he wasn't going to rip it out and eat it whole. I sympathetically stroked his hair with one hand and very slowly took the gun out of his cooperating hand with the other. I laid it on the shower floor and guided him to a standing position. We walked arm and arm out of the bathroom, through the bedroom and down the hall to the family room. We sat on the couch and were calmly talking about a visit with the children at his grandparents' house in the morning when there was a knock at the door. Dad opened the door and 5 or 6 police officers came busting in with their rifles in position. I looked up, made eye contact with one of the officers and said, "It's about time, I already have him calmed down. His gun is in the shower in the master bedroom."

The officers took Chris outside under the carport to talk with him. After a while one of the officers called me outside and informed me Chris told them he broke in because he didn't believe the children were safe at my parents' house. I started to get angry because he knew as well as I did, it was a crock of shit. He knew he had to say it so they wouldn't take him to jail. I motioned to one of the officers to talk to him privately, slowly taking a few steps away and told him Chris was addicted to crystal meth and was very dangerous. Glancing around, I noticed a used needle and syringe by the trash cans and brought it to the officers' attention. I explained this kind of behavior had been going on for quite some time and if they would just call downtown they would find a long list of charges pending against him already. But it was as if they had decided before they even called me outside they were going to let him go no matter what I said. Then what they told me next absolutely infuriated me. One of the officers told me to go inside and pack an overnight bag for my baby boy because they were going to let him take Christopher with him. I protectively blurted out, "Over my dead body! After all the havoc he just caused tonight, you're not taking him to jail?" He shook his head no in answer to my stare and I felt my blood begin to boil. The officer told me, he was just trying to see his kids and because no one was actually hurt there would be no charges filed. I was furious and turned to go in the house to tell my parents what was happening when I was stopped by the locked door. My emotions were all over the place as I looked Chris in the eyes and blurted out, "You better get a good job because I'm going to sue your ass good for child support! Turning back to face the door I yelled, "Open this fucking door!" as I pounded on it. I didn't mean it. I'm not like that and I regretted it the very moment I said it but I couldn't tell Chris that, ever. He would see it as me being submissive to him again and I couldn't have it. He had to see me as more confident. It was really more of a statement of authority so he knew I was taking back control of myself. My dad opened the door and I went in. I took a deep breath and told him what the officers said. He said, "No way" and told the officers he would be pressing breaking and entering charges. Once again the officers stunned us and told us those charges wouldn't stick because he didn't steal anything. So my dad asked what charges should be pressed considering all the damage Chris did and they said the best they could do would be malicious destruction of property. Finally, those were the charges pressed and they took him to jail.

Chapter 13

As sad as it sounds, I hoped Chris would stay behind bars for a while. Maybe then he would get clean and start to think straight so he could see he needed to abandon the drugs if he wanted a better life. Ironically, the timing couldn't have been more perfect since I had secretly been very worried about Chris showing up at my divorce party and ruining everything. The next week flew by and before I knew it, it was time to celebrate the end of my first marriage which in hindsight, probably never should have happened. Everyone in my family was gone as planned and I had to pick Juliana up from the airport. It was a quick trip since we lived right across Paradise Rd. from the airport. I got Juliana settled in and started to set up for the party. I only invited a handful of friends and a new friend from down the street, Meg and her husband. Of course Patti came and she brought her new boyfriend, Tom. I had plugged a watermelon with a bottle of rum the night before going on a suggestion from one of the invited guests. It was a big hit.

We were all having a good time when the doorbell rang. My heart sank as I secretly hoped it wasn't Chris who once again was bailed out of jail so quickly. Much to my surprise it was his brother Chuck and he had brought practically the whole gang of their neighborhood friends. He said, "I know we weren't invited but when you told me you were having a divorce party I knew we would all want to celebrate with you. We're all just as happy you and the kids are out of that situation as you are. Is it ok if we stay for a while?" I was touched and had become attached to them as friends each in their own way while Chris and I were married. Half of them were in our wedding party and I knew they were harmless so I agreed to let them in. Boy, let me tell you, those boys knew how to party. It wasn't long before they were climbing up on the roof to jump in the pool.

Suddenly I saw Megs' husband, Steve was looking around like he lost one of their 2 small children they brought with them. I started on my way over to see what he was looking for when he yelled, "Who stole my coke?" My mouth dropped open as I quickly ran to him and told him they had to leave. They knew everything I had just gone through with my ex-husband and the drugs so why would they think it was ok to bring cocaine to the party?

I brought Steve to Meg in the kitchen and insisted she take him home. He was pretty drunk when they arrived and continued to have more drinks throughout the evening. She told me she didn't know what he was talking about. He didn't have any cocaine but agreed to take him home since he was ready to fall over. Soon the night drew to a close as the guests left one by one. All in all, it was a great night. The next morning Juliana and I went for breakfast before I dropped her at the airport. It was a short 2 day visit but it was worth it as it fed my soul to see my best friend again. I hurried home to clean up before my family returned home.

It wasn't long before Chris was released from jail and his harassment began again. My dad decided the children and I should be hidden somewhere Chris would never look to find us. At the time he was working in telemarketing and his secretary Debbie who was about my age lived alone so he proposed a deal to her. He would pay her rent if she would let the children and I stay with her for a while and she agreed. I guess he thought if he could just hide us out somewhere for a while things would settle down and everything would be ok. I had no job or money so I was in no position to argue or refuse the help my parents gave me even if I didn't agree. The bottom line was I was putting all of them in harm's way living with them so the children and I had to go. Chris would never stop coming to their house if he knew we were there.

On our first night after the children were bathed and tucked in, Debbie and I sat down to talk as she poured us each a glass of wine. We felt pretty comfortable with each other and before we knew it we began to share our stories. She was about 3 months into a new relationship after her divorce and her new beau wanted her to move in with him. She said she was crazy about him and thought she probably would, she just didn't want to rush into it. Her thoughts were to hand over the apartment to me if she did and asked if I was interested. I reminded her it was only our first night there and I had no idea what was happening the next day let alone the near future. We laughed and she agreed.

The next morning I took the children to the pool thinking I might run into someone who lives in the complex and babysits so I could start working. Dad told me one of the salesmen in his office needed a secretary and he was pretty sure I could get the job so I knew I better get busy making arrangements for the children because he would expect me to start as soon as possible once he cleared it with Matz. I put our belongings on an empty table, put suntan lotion on the children then we headed to the steps. I noticed a woman sitting on the edge of the pool as she watched some children splash around. She introduced herself to me as the children and I eased our way into the water. It was as though it was meant to be. She was the complex managers' wife, Carol and she *did* babysit. She told me her price and pointed out which building they lived in and which children in the pool were hers and Mike's. We talked a bit about ourselves and our children to get familiar with one another. I was finally starting to feel a little relief, like maybe everything would work out.

Dad called that evening to tell me Matz was very excited to have a secretary and couldn't wait to meet me. He asked if I could start the next day and was very surprised when I told him yes, I already secured a babysitter right here in the complex. It was so convenient to drive over a couple of apartment buildings, drop the kids off and head to work. We started at 5am because we had to call the east coast as early as possible to catch the store owners when they weren't so busy yet. Us secretaries would dial the numbers and get the owners on the line then call our salesman to recite their pitch. Dad picked me up and dropped me off the first few days but then decided it was somewhat inconvenient for me to hang around sometimes more than an hour for him to finish up so he asked if I would mind carpooling with Debbie if she didn't mind. I agreed but after only a couple of weeks Debbie asked me if I would mind being there by myself with the children. She was ready to move in with her boyfriend. I was very scared of Chris finding us and I didn't want her to get hurt. I thought it would be better that way so I told her I didn't mind at all if that's what she wanted to do. It was a tiny, furnished studio apartment so she only had to pack her clothes and a small amount of personal items and she was gone. It was like she couldn't wait to get out of there. I figured the more she found out about my story the more scared she got. I think she was as nervous about Chris finding us as I was and I couldn't blame her. I often wondered what my dad was thinking to involve her knowing how violent and dangerous the situation was. I think he was just desperate to get me out of his house before Chris instigated another perilous situation. I was very scared one or more of my family members were going to get hurt or killed. My being there was putting them all in danger. Problem was, once Debbie left I had no way to get to work. Dad suggested we talk to Uncle Ronny and Aunt Rita about possibly loaning me one of their cars.

Aunt Rita had been in a horrible accident years ago when I was a child in Chicago and she vowed never to drive again. Uncle Ronny was a race car driver in his younger days and they had several cars they never drove. Dad and I asked them about a car and without hesitation they said yes. How ironic they would give me the orange Datsun they had loaned Chris and I when we went to California for his so-called job interview. I was nervous Chris might recognize it in the parking lot but beggars can't be choosers. I thanked them and left with the car.

After Debbie left I had no one to talk to at night when the children went to bed. I was alone with my thoughts and my broken spirit. I was a mess and didn't even realize it. I didn't have time to feel sorry for myself though. I had to stay strong for my babies. I thought I was doing a good job at it but my heart was broken and all I could do was to ask God why? Why wouldn't Chris just stop doing drugs? How could he not see the drugs were making him evil? When will it finally stop? It hurt so bad to think he loved the drugs more than his family.

ONE NIGHT I WAS TALKING ON the phone with my mom. She told me Chuck kept calling wanting to know where the children and I were and if we were ok so I decided to call him and put his mind at ease. He was so happy to hear my voice and demanded to know where we were, so he could come and see us. He promised he wouldn't tell Chris of our location as he knew how dangerous things were so I told him. We were actually in the same neighborhood as my parents and Grandma and Grandpa McGaughey whom he and Chris were still living with. I told him he had to come over after the children were asleep because I knew he was going to want to talk about everything going on and I didn't want them to hear any more about it if possible. He said he was going to go home, shower and have dinner after work the next day and then come over.

It was hard to fall asleep as I anticipated Chucks' visit. I wanted to believe he wouldn't tell Chris where we were but he *was* his brother. Is it possible I was too quick to trust Chuck with our location? What if he told Chris where we were or what if he brought Chris with him? Oh no! What did I do? I was getting very nervous and kept looking out the window to see if Chris was lurking outside waiting to pounce. After a while of pacing the floor I tried to calm myself down. Take a deep breath I told myself. Just lie down and try to go to sleep. Chuck has been on my side through all this knowing his brother was out of his mind on drugs so I decided to trust my gut and get some rest.

THE NEXT DAY FLEW BY AND before I knew it I was putting the children to bed. They had a full day of playing in the pool and running around outside in the fresh air. After dinner and their bath I knew it wouldn't be long before they were sound asleep. Soon I heard their tiny, soft snoring. I was really on edge hoping Chuck wasn't going to have Chris with him. I heard a car door close and peeked out the window. There was Chuck and his childhood friend, Steve, walking toward the door. Chuck was holding a single red rose in his hand. I said hello to them as I opened the door and put my finger over my puckered lips to instruct them to be quiet as to not wake the children. Chuck stepped in while

Steve gave me a hug, said he was glad to see we were alright and left. Chuck handed me the rose then leaned in for a big hug. I pointed to the corner of the small studio apartment by the window to show him the children were sleeping. He walked over to them and looked down at their makeshift bed I laid down for them with sleeping bags and blankets. He could see for himself they were safe and sound.

"Come sit down," I told Chuck as I patted the chair beside mine in the tiny dining area. He sat and gently took my chin in his hand turning my face toward him. He said, "I need to tell you something important. I have been keeping a secret from you for a long time and it's time you should know." I told him if he was going to tell me about another cheating escapade of his brothers' I didn't want to hear it. All the times I already knew about were quite enough and it didn't even matter anymore. He assured me it wasn't about Chris at all.

I watched as he picked up the rose from the table and began to run it gently down the side of my face as he professed his love for me. He confessed he had been in love with me for the last two years I was married to his brother and it was killing him to see how horrible Chris was treating me. I was stunned to say the least as I never had the slightest idea he felt this way. It was then I knew for sure Chuck was not going to tell Chris where we were. He was in protection mode. He said he had to see us with his own eyes to know for sure we were safe. He leaned in to kiss me and I couldn't help but return the kiss. I was so lonely, vulnerable and broken. I needed so badly right then to feel I was loved, to be held and told everything was going to be ok. Chuck did just that as if he knew exactly what he had to say and do to win me over.

He had wanted it for so long and was so happy I returned his kiss instead of pushing him away. We were both overcome with emotion each with our own separate needs and were soon on the bed taking our clothes off. I was lost and wasn't thinking. I just went with it driven only by my intense emotional need to feel loved again. We quickly had sex and got dressed right after as I was worried the children might wake up. I didn't want them to see us like that together.

Chuck was so happy he was grinning from ear to ear. I wasn't too sure what to make of it all because I immediately felt like something wasn't right. I told him I thought he better go and he agreed as he blurted out a plan to see us the next day. I think as far as he was concerned we were then a couple. I was confused about my feelings and tried to make sense of it but I just kept coming back to how good it felt to be held and feel loved again.

Things were calm for a while and Chris had stopped calling my parents' house looking for me so we moved back in with them. Chuck would come over to the house a few times a week just to hang out and watch television with us after work. The children really enjoyed spending time with their uncle again. They had missed him as much as he missed them. One night after everyone went to sleep we ended up in my room and had sex again. It felt awkward and I asked him to leave while we were getting dressed as I was once again feeling strange and confused about our relationship. Something just didn't feel right.

Of course it wasn't long before Chris called the house looking for me. I just happened to answer when he did. He ran through the whole story again of how worried he was when he couldn't find me. Honestly, like it isn't the hundredth time I've heard it. I felt annoyed and had gained a little courage back so I just jumped in and asked, "What do you want Chris?" He started by telling me he just came back to his grandparents' house and he couldn't believe how happy Chuck was acting. He said, "I think he's in love or something. He's on cloud nine. Singing and dancing around the house and he's got a permanent smile on his face, he's grinning from ear to ear." I secretly felt flattered but then immediately like I just got punched in the gut. I felt so nauseated and it made me see the reality of how we were doing Chris wrong. How did this not even enter my mind before? Maybe it was part of not feeling right about being with Chuck but I just couldn't put my finger on it before. I felt so bad. If he only knew Chucks' new love was *me!* Oh my God! I wondered if I should just tell him then. I think he should hear it from me but I was afraid of how he was going to take the news and what he was going to do. I also knew once he found out it would only confirm his suspicions he had for a while about Chuck and I even though nothing had ever happened between us while Chris and I were married. I decided in a moment it was better to just come clean so I told him. He was furious to say the least and he got the crazy notion in his head our son Christopher was Chucks' child, not his at all. I told him he was crazy and assured him I had never cheated on him adding I wished he could say the same. The brothers' relationship was never the same again.

It had only been a couple of months when I realized I loved Chuck but I wasn't in love with him. He was like a brother to me and I knew it would never work between us. I couldn't love him like he deserved, it just didn't feel right. I had to break up with him but I knew it was going to break his heart. I asked him to come over one night after everyone went to bed. I explained I finally realized I loved him as a brother and not how he should be loved in a relationship. I apologized and told him nothing romantic ever should have happened between us and how I felt it was not the right thing to do to his brother. I told him I never meant to hurt him and I shouldn't have just jumped into things with him when I was still so messed up from my marriage and divorce. He was true to his nature being very understanding and actually agreed although I could see through his tough exterior he was devastated. He used to sing the song "For the Longest Time" to me and dubbed it "our song" when he told me he had waited for the longest time to make me his girl. As the song says, he told me in the beginning he was willing to take his chances and go for it. I told him I would love for him to remain close to the children and he could see them whenever he wanted. He thanked me with tears in his eyes, gave me a hug and started toward the door. I impulsively blurted out, "Please don't hate me." He turned around, looked me in the eyes and said, "I could never hate you. You're the love of my life." Tears began to stream down both our faces as he gently opened the door, walked out and closed it behind him. I locked the door and went to my bedroom falling on the bed as I balled like a baby. My heart was heavy and I knew our relationship would never be the same.

Chapter 14

I QUIT WORKING WITH MY DAD to take a job offer at Zody's Department Store as a cashier. It was a few more hours but not quite full time which I was still looking for. I thought it might turn into fulltime but I was still hoping I would hear from one of the many banks I applied at. At least I didn't have to wake the children up in the middle of the night to go to the babysitter anymore because I had to be to work by 5am. I worked the evenings and weekends so the children could stay at home with my mom.

I kept busy with work and the children and told myself I didn't need a man in my life, it only complicated things. I stopped taking the birth control pill knowing I wasn't going to be having sex with anyone any time soon. I needed to focus on getting on my feet without Chris. It was all on me. My children's happiness depended on me. I also didn't want to live with my parents very long. I will always be thankful for their help but I needed to make a home for me and my children.

I was happy the holiday season was approaching. In the retail business it always means more hours. Yay! I hated being away from my children more but I loved the bigger paychecks. It was more money to put away toward our own place. It was amazing how it boosted my confidence and gave me back my independence. It empowered me. I started to feel a little stronger and more self-assured. I felt hopeful I could rebuild my self-esteem and self-worth. I had to keep pushing myself so I could get stronger and be the best mother I could be. I would give myself pep talks and tell myself, "You *can* do this." I was feeling more optimistic about the future.

Halloween came and everyone at work dressed up. I was a punk rocker complete with a green Mohawk. We had a lot of fun and a lot of food at our pot luck lunch. It had only been a few weeks and I already got a promotion to head cashier. I started my rounds of collecting the drops from my cashiers near the end of my shift when I was surprised by an all too familiar voice behind me say, "Hi Karen. I found you again." I froze for a few seconds in utter amazement. When I turned around Chris was there looking overly anxious to see my reaction. It stroked his monumental ego to see the astonishment on my face. All of a sudden my hands started to tremble as my stomach began to surge. Immediately the fear he had instilled in me came rushing back. I could feel goose bumps popping up all over my body while he stared me down with his usual arrogant condescending grin. He told me he just wanted to stop in to let me know he knows where I work. Then he proceeded to tell me his grandparents wouldn't let him stay with them any longer because he kept threatening to kill them if they didn't stay out of his business. He said he didn't have any money and begged me to get him a furnished studio apartment for a week or two so he wouldn't be on the street anymore. He promised he wouldn't ask me to pay for any more than the first two weeks and as soon as he got a job he would pay me back. He went on to say he already found a reasonable place only a few blocks from my parents' house. He said, "Think about it and I'll come back tomorrow" then he turned and left.

Was that some kind of threat? I thought, "I just wanted to let you know I know where you work." What the hell? I hate when he does those things. I knew if I didn't pay for his apartment he would continue to come to my job and cause problems. I told myself I had to stay strong and not let him intimidate me anymore or at least not let him see he was. It was obvious he still wasn't off the drugs. He looked creepier than the last time I saw him. I took a deep breath then blew it out. I finished my shift with thoughts of spending time with my beautiful babies when I got home. I knew they would be in their costumes anxiously waiting to go trick or treating.

The Haunting Sliver of Light

As I trick or treated with the children all I could think about was Chris' unexpected visit and the favor he asked of me. I hated to think of taking money out of my moving fund to get Chris an apartment especially since I knew I would never get it back but I kept thinking about how he had nowhere to go. He *is* the father of my children and I felt sorry for him being on the street. I didn't want to be with him anymore but I didn't wish anything bad for him either. I decided this would be the last time I help him and I would make it clear to him he was on his own after the two weeks was up.

It was hard for me to fall asleep as I kept wondering if paying for the apartment was going to give him mixed messages. I know how he thinks and I didn't want him thinking there was a chance of us reuniting. I would have to make it clear to him when we went to get the apartment. There was no way I was just going to give him the money so he could blow it on drugs and have no apartment to show for it. He came to Zody's the next day to get my answer. I told him I would do it after my shift was over and to meet me at the complex.

After I paid for the first two weeks we went up to the second floor apartment to check it out. It wasn't but a few minutes later when he asked me if he could have a visit with the children. I agreed but told him I didn't trust him yet and I would have to stay with them as he only had supervised visitations. He said he understood and he would take whatever he could get.

I went to my parents' house to pick up the children and told my mom I was taking them to visit their father. I let her know he had a small apartment down the street and after I packed up the diaper bag we left.

Only a short while in the apartment, Chris asked if we could spend the night knowing I didn't work the next day. He said he would sleep on the couch and the children and I could have the bed. I told him if we did it was only so he could have more time with the children and it didn't mean I was interested in reconciling with him. He said he understood. I told him I was going to run downstairs where I saw a pay phone to call my mom to let her know we were spending the night. She was a little worried but agreed it was good for the children to have some time with their father. I assured her there was no thought on my part of a reconciliation and we would be home the next day.

When I went back up to the apartment it warmed my heart to see my babies laughing and having fun playing with their father. It was a little awkward but all in all we had a nice visit. Chris didn't do any drugs as far as I could see and he was actually attentive to the children all evening. Once the children were bathed and tucked in, he jokingly suggested we have sex but I shut him down immediately.

The Haunting Sliver of Light

In the morning we went for breakfast and the grocery store so I could buy him a few things. We carried the groceries up to the apartment and put them away while the children played with some of their toys I brought with us. Chris was actually very cordial and non-aggressive which I started to believe may be a ploy to get back in my good graces but I decided not to second guess anything. I just wanted the visit to be pleasant for him and the children hoping he would see the beauty of what he was missing out on. I even gave him some compliments regarding his interaction with the children trying to encourage him. I wanted to make a point of letting him know I wanted our children to know their father and have him in their lives even though him and I would not be together. I told him he could still be a good father even if we weren't a couple and the children needed him in their lives. It seemed as though I might finally be getting through to him. At least it appeared as though he was thinking about it. We all enjoyed our visit but soon it was time to head home. We said our good byes and Chris thanked me for everything. I left feeling hopeful.

WITH CHRISTMAS WELL ON ITS WAY, we were very busy at the store and we were hiring. I recommended my girlfriend Meg from down the street for a position at the snack bar and she got the job.

We would sometimes work the same shift which allowed us more time together and we became closer. We began to hang out more and our children became good friends too. It was nice to have a friend close by. I really missed having Nancy right across the street.

One day Patti called me to catch up and was telling me her father accepted a job offer in Germany with a 2 year contract. Since they didn't want to sell their house she decided to stay and take care of the house. She was planning a little going away party for them and invited me. Everyone was meeting at the lounge show at the Marina Hotel on the Strip where she and I used to go to have a couple drinks and listen to the band play. I loved her parents and told her I would definitely be there.

Patti had an assortment of appetizers to pick on and a section of tables already reserved when I got there. The guests started to fill the chairs and the party was in full swing. There was laughing, crying, dancing and hugging, lots of reminiscing and heartfelt toasts made to bid farewell to Jim and Ann. As the night wore on I couldn't help but notice the drummer in the band had been keeping an eye on me most of the night. I tried not to make eye contact with him and kept looking away. I didn't want him to think I was interested in him or in getting to know him. It was getting late and most of the guests had left leaving a lot of empty chairs. The lead singer announced they were going to take a break and the next thing I knew the drummer sat in the empty chair to my right. He said, "Hi, I'm Quinn. I'm guessing you're a local because I've seen you in here on and off for a while now. Haven't you noticed me admiring you?" I looked around for Patti to rescue me but she was busy packing up the leftovers, gathering the gifts and talking to the few remaining guests. I was left to my own devices.

I smiled and said, "Hi, I'm Karen. And yes, *I did* notice you looking at me several times while you were playing but I thought…" Before I could say another word he interrupted me saying, "You're beautiful and I'd like to get to know you better. Are you staying until our last set? There's only one more, it's about an hour long." I told him it was getting late and I had to get home to my children. I never used my children as an excuse for anything but I was hoping it would make him back off. It really wasn't an excuse, it was the truth. I started to tell him I wasn't interested in a relationship then he interrupted me again. He said his car was in the shop and he was hoping I would give him a ride home to give us a chance to talk and get to know each other. He said he wasn't looking for a relationship either, just a friend. I started to feel bad about how I was thinking I had to get rid of him and began to consider his request. It would be after midnight when he was done working, it's kind of late. I wanted to be home by midnight. Then he made it a point to tell me he had no one else to call and would probably end up taking the bus if I couldn't give him a ride. He seemed harmless and it was cold outside so I agreed.

After all the guests had left I helped Patti and her parents carry everything out to the car. I told them good night and let Patti know I was waiting to give Quinn a ride home. She gave me a big smile and wriggled her eyebrows. I assured her I wasn't interested in any hanky panky and it was only a ride. We hugged, I told her to be safe and I would be in touch soon. I went back in and sat down at my table to wait for him. Listening to the music I thought, "What am I doing? I don't even know this guy. But how bad can he be if he's letting me see where he lives right off the bat? I'll just drop him off and be on my way home." I could feel his eyes on me while I'm having this conversation with myself trying again not to make eye contact with him. I don't want him to think I'm flirting with him or anything of the sort. He was so not my type either and if anything grew between us I already knew it would only be friendship. Finally they were announcing their last song of the night. I finished the last few swigs of my drink and gathered my smokes and keys as I put my coat on.

He said good night to the other band members and we walked out to the car. All the way to his house he made small talk but I really didn't care because for the first time in my life I didn't know what to say. It actually felt a little awkward but I took a deep breath and told myself to give him a chance. He might end up being a good guy and a great friend. He talked about the guys in the band and their plans to change their show a little in the New Year. He kept the conversation light and funny making me laugh out loud a few times. By the time we pulled up in front of his house he had made me feel pretty comfortable. I thought to myself, he *did* seem like a decent guy.

He asked me to come in for a drink and was a little offended when I declined. He insisted saying it was the least he could do for the ride home and it would give us a little more time to get to know each other. I hesitated and told him I had two drinks at the party which was my limit. "Come on," he said, "you don't have to have alcohol. I have water and soda too. I don't expect you to stay too long, how about just 30 more minutes?" Against my better judgment I gave in.

As we were walking in the door he put his finger to his puckered lips and said, "Sshh, we have to be quiet because my roommate is sleeping" as he pointed to a closed door on the other side of the huge living room. I nodded my head yes as my attention was drawn to all the autographed photographs of movie stars on the wall above the couch.

He headed to his bedroom putting up one finger. I assumed he wanted to change into something more comfortable than the suit he wears for work. As I was checking out the pictures I heard the stereo go on and the song "What's Love Got to do with it" started playing. I was confused because I thought the stereo was a little too loud if someone was sleeping in the next room. Just then a nervous feeling began to conjure in my stomach and I got an anxious pins and needles feeling all over. When I turned toward his bedroom to inquire about the music I was greeted by him in nothing but a thong coming at me with a vengeance. He was very tall and easily overpowered me. Before I knew it he had me pinned down on the couch and was literally ripping the clothes off of my body! I tried to push him off while I was screaming for him to stop. It suddenly became apparent there was no roommate in the other room. There was no one to hear my screams. If there was someone in there surely they would have come out by now with all the noise.

He succeeded in getting me totally naked all the while holding me down with one arm across my chest as he lay on top of me. I was kicking and trying to push him off of me but to no avail. He was practically shoving his tongue down my throat making it hard to breathe as he pressed his mouth against mine, hard. Then he told me to listen to the words of the song so I understood love had nothing to do with sex as he pulled his thong off to reveal his growing penis. He started kissing and licking my body on his way down to perform oral sex on me. I waited until he was positioned just right then pushed his shoulders back with my feet as hard as I could to get away from him. I scooted away and noticed he was on his back on the floor with his bulging penis the highest point of his body. It was like a skyscraper in the penis world! I was young and hadn't had very many sexual partners but I had never seen a penis so long before! It seemed as though my forcefulness only invigorated him, he was turned on even more. Now I was really scared. He came back at me and flipped me around gathering my wrists behind my back and forcefully pulled me to my feet shoving me into his bedroom where I fell to the floor. I went to get up but he pushed me down on my hands and knees ordering me to stay down. He held me down with one foot on my back as he watched himself stroke his enormous erection. I couldn't move. Then he jumped into position behind me driving his penis inside me. I tensed up knowing it was going to hurt.

I watched him in the mirrored doors of the closet as he kept thrusting himself in and out with one hand squeezing the back of my neck for control. He looked insane! He was admiring his physique numb to the fact I was crying and was not a participating partner. Every time I tried to push him or pull away from him he squeezed my neck tighter. He shoved his penis in even harder then I felt him gather my hair together and wrap it around his hand just like Chris used to do. I instinctively went into submissive mode as the fear grew inside me and just prayed for him to finish. At that moment I realized it was all a plan to get me there. I don't even think he *had* a car. It also became obvious I wasn't his first victim. It all seemed so routine to him. It appeared he got off on watching himself in the act and had an insatiable appetite for being in control. He was riding me like a stallion to the finish line with me being an insignificant object. All I could muster the courage to say was, "Please don't cum inside me. I will get pregnant." No sooner did I get the words out he gave me one last intense thrust and he was done. He held his position while his throbbing penis released his orgasm inside me and I could feel the demon sperm cells swimming up my canal looking for a mate. I was waiting to see what his next move would be unsure if he was going to allow me to leave and it scared me. As he pulled himself out of me I began to imagine my fate. What if there were other girls who were locked in the room he had pointed at? Was he going to add me to his growing harem?

I was extremely surprised when he got up and held out his hand to help me up. It was as if it was all completely normal to him. He motioned for me to go with him into the living room and even looked around picking up my clothes and handed them to me. I quickly tried to put them on so I could get the hell out of there. He put his thong back on and even walked me out to the car then asked when he could see me again. UH, NEVER, I thought but I didn't want to upset him, I wasn't out of there yet. Truth be known, I was shocked as hell he even let me go. I was thinking by the rough nature of the sex he had other plans for me.

I thanked God in my head and told Quinn I would see him at the lounge show in a couple of days. He shook his head affirmatively and started back toward the house as he waved goodbye. I had to pacify him so I could leave but I had no intentions of EVER going back to the lounge show or seeing him ever again! What a freak!

I backed up and drove home essentially in my bra and panties. He had ripped my dress and nylons so badly they wouldn't even stay on my body. I cried hard all the way home and was so mad at myself I didn't go with my first instinct when I said no. I should have just gone home. I was pretty sure I had just gotten pregnant. I remembered how fast I got pregnant with Christopher when I had my breast reduction surgery and had to go off the pills. So it was already confirmed in my mind because I had stopped taking my pills and was very fertile. I was so upset. I couldn't bear to think of having a child with that maniac. I planned an abortion on my way home. I just didn't know how long I had to wait to do it. I already felt like I had the spawn of Satan growing inside me. Suddenly I had to stop and lean out the door to puke. The more I thought about it the sicker I felt.

THE MORNING SICKNESS STARTED WITHIN A week and confirmed my worst suspicions. I didn't want to waste any time so I got on the phone and called a facility to make the appointment. The young lady asked how far along I was and was shocked when I said one week. "Oh honey it's too early. You're going to have to wait. It will take a couple more weeks for the fertilized egg to reach the womb," she said. She sounded firm and precise, she knew her stuff. Then she threw a date at me several weeks out and told me I had to bring someone to drive me home. She ended with, "Also it will cost $300.00 and check in half an hour before your appointment time, any questions?" I said, "No. Thank you." She said, "Have a nice day" and we hung up.

I couldn't even afford the abortion. I had already taken money from our moving fund to get Chris an apartment and was still trying to replenish it. What am I going to do? I did not want to go see Quinn and ask him for money. I watched my beautiful angels play and questioned myself about ending the pregnancy. After all it was a part of me too but all I could think about was if I would end up treating him or her different from April and Christopher because this pregnancy was forced upon me? It wouldn't be fair to the child to grow up knowing it and yearning for his or her father. There was also no way I wanted to have to see Quinn to raise a child together. I had 2 babies to worry about already and I would never get a good job being pregnant. Then it suddenly popped in my mind how it would also give Chris ammunition to take me to court for custody of the children, painting me as an unfit mother who is out sleeping around. It was very overwhelming! I knew it had to be done.

I couldn't tell my parents. I knew my mom would try to talk me into keeping the baby and I just couldn't bear it. I had to tell someone though, someone I could trust so I called Patti. I told her I had to discuss something very important with her and it had to remain a secret. She could tell it was of an urgent nature and told me to come right over. I left the children with my mom telling her Patti needed me for an emergency and I would be right back. When I walked in Patti's house I broke down in tears and hugged her tight. I told her what happened and I was never going back to the lounge show. I told her I couldn't bring myself to look at him let alone tell him I was pregnant or raise a child with him. I didn't want anyone else knowing or trying to talk me out of the abortion. My mind was made up. It was what I needed to do and she said she understood. I asked if I could borrow the money and promised to make payments to pay her back. She knew I would and agreed.

As the day drew near I still didn't have a ride. I couldn't ask Patti to take a day off work for me. She already helped tremendously by paying for the procedure. I was desperate but there was no one else I trusted enough to tell then I thought of Chuck. I knew he would do anything for me. I figured it was worth a try so I called him and asked if I could see him. It had been a while since we saw each other. He did not call or come over one time to see the children since I had broken up with him but he immediately said yes, he would come over straight from work.

We were getting ready for dinner as I anxiously paced back and forth checking out the window to see his car. Finally he pulled up and parked in front of the house. I yelled out, "I'm going out front for a few minutes, be right back" as I quickly ran out the door and jumped in the front seat next to him. I had to be quick and to the point. It was so emotional I broke down crying immediately and told him I was pregnant. I made it clear I wasn't keeping the baby. It would just make things much more difficult.

It had been months since we were together so the thought never occurred to me he might think the child was his until he asked. I assured him it was not his child but couldn't bear to tell him what happened. I had already thought of the consequences of Chris and/or Chuck finding out what happened. I knew both of them would seek the guy out and torture him if not kill him. I couldn't live with it especially if they ended up in prison as a result. There was no reason either of them had to know. What I didn't think of was if I didn't tell Chuck what happened he was led to believe it was his child. He was the only guy I was with after my husband and he knew it. I thought it would erase all doubt in his mind if I just reminded him I was on the pill while we were together. I didn't stop taking the pill until after I broke it off with him. He said it didn't matter since I had made up my mind. He said he understood my position and he supported me 100%. I told him I already scheduled the appointment but needed someone to come along because I wouldn't be able to drive home. He said he would stay with me all day if I needed him to. I told him what day the appointment was so he could get the day off work and it was settled. Whew! I felt a little more relieved knowing everything was in order. I thanked him, gave him a hug and ran back in the house.

As we were eating dinner I was playing out the whole thing in my mind. Oh no, I forgot I needed someone to watch the children while I was having the procedure done. Shit! I had to tell and involve another person and who would it be I asked myself. I thought of Meg and hoped she wasn't scheduled to work that day. After dinner the kids and I took a walk to her house so I could talk to her. She was totally supportive. She told me she would schedule the day off and keep the kids all day. Thank God! Ok, everything was set.

The day came and went unnoticed by everyone in my family. I had Chuck drop me off at Megs' house and he left. I was in a lot of pain and knew I couldn't go home as it would be obvious something was wrong so Meg told me to just hang out at her house for a while. She suggested I go lay down but the pain was too intense to sleep. I had to call the facility to ask if it was normal. The young lady who answered the phone put a nurse on the line. She said, "It's most likely just gas. It should pass within a couple of hours. Give it a little time and you'll feel much better. If you don't, call back and the doctor will see you."

I asked Meg about work to get my mind off the pain. She took me on a journey to show how she felt about each and every person she worked with at the snack bar. She made me laugh and bend and before I knew it one and half hours had passed. Just as I noticed the time I started passing gas like you wouldn't believe. The nurse was right. I felt much better physically but I couldn't stop crying. It was all very emotional.

Meg tried to comfort me with a hug and usher me to lie down but there was no sense in trying. I didn't want to sleep I just wanted to watch the children play. The tears welled up in my eyes as I tried to imagine if there was another child in the group. What would he or she look like? Be like? I felt such heartache over the abortion yet knew in my heart it's what I had to do. Suddenly Meg nudged my shoulder to give me some tissues. I mouthed the words thank you as I took them from her and wiped my face where the tears had dripped down my cheeks then patted my eyes dry.

We sat and watched the children hard at play and it made me realize I had to put it behind me and focus on the children I already had to be responsible for. I gave myself a couple of hours to grieve and it had to be enough. My children were relying on me to be there for them no matter what I was going through. I didn't have time to get depressed or let anything I had been through mess me up or hold me down. I had to be strong for my children and put them first. I told myself my feelings didn't matter and were not a priority.

Take some deep breaths I told myself, it's going to be ok. Meg asked if I was hungry yet and it sounded like a good idea to feed my belly, I was kind of hungry. We made a late lunch together and called the children in as we made plates for them and ourselves. As we enjoyed our lunch I told Meg I didn't want to live at my parents' house anymore. It was time the children and I were on our own but I couldn't afford our own apartment, not having a full time job yet. We had grown much closer and she suggested the children and I move in with her family. I kind of chuckled and said, "And where would we sleep?" She stood up and motioned for me to follow her as she took me up the spiral staircase in her living room to reveal a huge bedroom with a wall to wall closet and a private bathroom. It was empty and move in ready. I was very impressed. I never knew what was at the top of the spiral staircase and never had a reason to ask. I looked around and could picture where

I would put our beds, dressers and the children's toys. It seemed perfect and she could see I was grinning from ear to ear. She asked, "How does $300.00 a month sound?" I enthusiastically fired back with, "Are you kidding me? I can afford that on my income now without a fulltime job." I was so excited I hugged her and accepted. We went downstairs and I told her I would get back to her about a move in date. She assured me whatever day I settled on was fine with her.

I thanked Meg for everything after the kitchen was cleaned up and gathered our things. April and Christopher told their friends goodbye as I gave Meg another big thank you hug. We walked down to my parents' house where I thought the third degree would start. I tried to act like it was a normal day not to give anything away. So far it was working. Then when I began to unpack things from Christopher's diaper bag my mom noticed I had bought maxi pads instead of my usual tampons. She was curious enough to ask me about it. I had to tell her a little white lie and say I had a yeast infection so the doctor recommended I use pads and not tampons for a while. It satisfied her and all was good.

Chapter 15

THE FEELING OF A FULL BLADDER woke me to the consciousness of a new day. I could hear the children were awake as their angelic giggles tickled my ear drums. They added the pitter patter of their little feet as they ran down the hall and into my room jumping on the bed asking for breakfast. "We want pannycakes!" yelled Christopher. "Yeah," April added as her tiny tongue came out to lick her lips. 'Then pannycakes it is!' I said. We hopped off the bed and headed down the hall to the living room. I quickly changed Christopher's diaper and turned on the television to keep them occupied with their favorite, Sesame Street. "Mommy has to go potty. Watch your show and I will call you when breakfast is ready," I instructed as I hurried through the horse-shoe shaped house. Passing through the large den beside the kitchen before turning down the hallway to the bathroom I planned my strategy for the day. It was a beautiful morning and since it was my day off I could plan a whole day of fun with my babies. Maybe we'll go to the park for a while. Grandma, Grandpa, Uncle Kenny and Uncle Kevin were all at work so we had the day to ourselves. As I washed my hands I figured I'd let them decide.

I rounded the corner at the end of the hall and my heart sank when the kids came running through the den yelling, "Daddy's here!" Behind them was Chris walking toward me with his old friend 357 in his hand. They had heard his motorcycle pull up under the carport and vibrate the house. They knew it was their daddy so April opened the door. He told me he wasn't leaving without us and began yelling and asking me why I wanted the divorce. He didn't even remember we were already divorced and I wasn't about to remind him. He would have become even more enraged. The children hated when he yelled at me and would always run to the bedroom. They peeked out of the doorway as they saw him push me onto the couch and he proceeded to load his gun. I told the children to stay in the bedroom but once again Chris contradicted me and ordered them to come into the living room. They scurried in and climbed on my lap leaning into my chest for comfort.

He just kept waving the loaded gun around as he ranted and raved about the divorce. He told me he couldn't find a job and had to let the apartment I got for him go after the 2 weeks I paid for. He had been going from friend to friends' house and eventually ended up back at his grandparents' house because he ran out of options. He said they weren't too happy about him coming back since they could tell he was still using drugs but they were too afraid of him to tell him no because he threatened to kill whoever got in his way, including them.

Then he made his way into the kitchen and asked me if there was any beer in the fridge, knowing there never was. I answered no and suddenly the phone rang. My heart about jumped out of my chest! My hands were shaking uncontrollably as I reached for the phone and looked in the direction of the kitchen to see if he was watching me. I totally expected him to forbid me to answer the phone but he didn't say a word about it so I picked up the receiver and said, "Hello?" Much to my surprise I found Chuck on the other end. He was calling to see how I was feeling and it had been awhile since he last saw the children so he was hoping we could meet him for lunch. I hoped I would be able to alert Chuck so he could call the police. I started giving him crazy answers to his questions so he would realize Chris was there. A couple of minutes seemed like an hour then he finally said, "Oh my God, Chris is there, isn't he?" I answered with a simple "Yes." Thank God!! He asked me if he had his gun and I said yes! He said, "Oh my God! Stay calm! I'm calling the police right now!" and hung up.

Chris began to question who was on the phone. I tried to tell him it was the wrong number but he wasn't buying it. He said he knew it was Chuck, he could tell. I thought it would send him into a rage if I admitted it was Chuck so I kept denying it. After a few minutes of him insisting it was and saying I should just come clean about it, the phone rang again. It made me jump. I reached for the receiver with my trembling hand while watching him for reassurance that it was okay with him to do so. He nodded yes so I answered. It was the police dispatcher wanting to question me about the situation. She told me she had received a call of desperation from Chuck and said the SWAT team was on their way. She needed to know the layout of the house and what rooms everyone was in just in case the situation erupted into a shoot out! What? My heart was about pounding out of my chest. She then asked me if I thought Chris would come to the phone and talk to her. After a few minutes of whispering Chris came into the living room saying, "I know it's the cops isn't it?" I told him the dispatcher wanted to talk to him. Much to my surprise he calmly took the phone but within seconds he began to get very irate as the dispatcher told him to surrender by putting the gun in the living room window and walk out with his hands up. This infuriated him because he always had to be in control. Nobody told him what to do. He began to yell at the dispatcher telling her he wasn't going anywhere without me and the kids and the cops just needed to back off. The children and I were sobbing as they clung to me and struggled to stay still on my lap. Chris slammed the phone down and said they would have to kill him before he would surrender. I tried to reason with him and told him he would never see us again if he turned it into a bloodbath.

Then we heard a policeman over the megaphone tell him to surrender and come out with his arms up in the air. "We might all end up dead" I sobbed as I pleaded for him to put the gun in the window and walk out calmly. I even told him I didn't want to see him get hurt either. He sat in the blue overstuffed chair as he contemplated what to do. The phone rang again making all of us jump to our feet. This time Chris answered the phone. It was the police dispatcher. She asked him again to surrender and tried to tell him he didn't want the situation to end up with them having to call an ambulance or worse yet, the coroner. He finally told her he would surrender and he slowly walked over to the window, put the gun on the windowsill and headed for the door. He opened the door and started ever so slowly down the driveway. When he reached the sidewalk he was swarmed with police officers and thrown facedown onto the street. I looked out to make sure they had him in handcuffs and saw he was still face down in the street with about 10 rifles pointed in his back. An officer came directly over to me to ask if the children and I were okay and right behind him was a news camera shoved in our faces. The children had stepped out of the house behind me and the newsman got a close up of April as I yelled, 'Get your camera out of here!"

Back in the house trying to calm myself and the children down, the police were filling out reports and asking all kinds of questions. I asked if the charges would be attempted murder, holding hostages or what. The officer said the charges would probably not be attempted murder and he wasn't sure what they would want to do with it downtown. Chuck peeked his head in the door. He had to see us with his own eyes. I ran over to hug him and thank him for calling the police. He knew it wasn't the right time for a visit and told me he was glad to see we were alright but he had to get back to work. I thanked him again and told him we would see him soon.

One of the officers got the gun out of the window and checked it. Guess what? No bullets! Then they told me the charges wouldn't stick anyway because the gun wasn't loaded when he made the threat. I was dumbfounded! "It's not possible," I said. "I watched him load the gun right in front of me!" Yet there were no bullets found in the gun or anywhere in the house. They checked his pockets and found no bullets. Nevertheless, they took him in to the station and booked him.

The next day I got a call from Detective Jackson, the lead detective on the case. He told me Chris' first night in jail he tried to strangle his cell mate so they had to put him in shackles and he would remain in shackles 24/7 in a private cell until they thought he could control himself. He also said, "Unless we find those bullets somewhere in the house, we don't have a case." Suddenly a light bulb went on in my head. "Is it possible he swallowed the bullets?" I asked thinking out loud. I continued, "He was in the kitchen for a while and asked for a beer. I know it sounds crazy but I wouldn't put it past him considering everything else. You don't know the half of it. Is it possible to give him x-rays to see if he swallowed the bullets?" Although he was kind of taken back by my question he sort of snickered then said he would look into it. He advised me to keep looking for the bullets and said he would be in touch.

Over the next couple of weeks Chris called the house regularly to rant and badger me about dropping the charges. On and off there were police officers coming by to ask more questions trying to put the case together. Every time they came to the house I asked them to please do something about Chris calling all the time but they insisted he wasn't able to make calls. Each time I assured them someone was giving him phone privileges because he was harassing us with phone calls day and night. Then finally one day when mom and I were talking with a police officer Chris called. I was never so happy to hear from him. Thank goodness! He started right off the bat talking about the coffins and the white slavery ring so I motioned to the officer to come to the phone and listen. Up until then they all thought I was a little looney with the stories I told them he was telling me.

Finally, it's about time an officer heard it with his own ears right from the horses' mouth. I turned the receiver so we could both hear Chris at the same time. The officers' eyes about popped out of his head then he rotated his hand encouraging me to keep him talking as he hastily scribbled down some notes on his pad of paper. He was so close to me I could feel his body heat as we stood cheek to cheek. He was so shocked his mouth dropped open. I could feel his breath on my face as he breathed in and out. He wanted me to keep Chris talking so I asked if he was at least feeling better since he hadn't had any drugs in weeks. To which he replied, "Karen, if you think I can't get drugs in here, you're crazy. This jail is loaded with criminals who can get anything you want smuggled in. I have a buddy across the hall from me and he slides his Bible across the floor to my cell on a regular basis." Since I didn't understand the point he was trying to make I asked, "What is that supposed to mean? How is his Bible getting you drugs?" We first heard his arrogant giggle followed by, "Ah, literally. Some of the pages are hollowed out so he can fit the drugs inside. The cops think he is just sharing his Bible. That's what they want to see, the criminals turn to Jesus and when you start reading the Bible they believe you're on your way to rehabilitation. I'm still getting high Karen, even in jail." I gasped and the officer gave out a muted grunt unintentionally. Chris caught on and asked, "There's a cop listening isn't there?" Before I could answer we heard him shout "FUCK" as he slammed down the phone.

The officer put his paper and pen away. He was absolutely astounded! He looked at me and said, "Ma'am, I have to be honest, we all owe you an apology. We thought you were making up these stories you've been telling us. Your husband is very good at manipulation, let me tell you. He led us to believe you were the one hooked on drugs and making up these stories. We have been coming here on and off specifically to see if we could trip you up and get conflicting stories but you have been very consistent the whole time. Not to mention, every officer who has been here questioning you has said you certainly don't appear to be strung out on drugs." I was so relieved. Maybe now, I thought, things would change. The tables have finally turned. Hopefully there wouldn't be any more harassing phone calls. I trusted the officer would go back to the police station and spread the news of how he actually heard it straight from Chris' mouth himself. He said he would look into things immediately and left as though he was on a mission.

Only a few days later when I was watching cartoons with the children, Christopher came over to me and went to hand me something. I extended my open hand assuming he wanted me to play soldiers with him again. I was shocked when I saw him drop a few bullets into my hand. I immediately grabbed him, stood up and swung him around. "Mommy loves you so much! Where did you get these from?" I asked as I kissed his chubby little cheek a hundred times. I put him down so he could show me where he was pointing. He ran over to the large blue chair with the ottoman and shoved his little hand down in the crease of the chair where he hid his army soldiers and toy cars. To my amazement he pulled out a couple more bullets. Then April piped in and said, "Daddy told Gitifer to hide those bullets last time he was here." I was never so happy to see bullets. I told the children they cracked the case and I was so proud of them. I hugged and kissed them over and over. They got so excited and started dancing around the living room. I had to call Detective Jackson right away.

He was thrilled when I told him Christopher found the bullets. He said he was very relieved because he was hard pressed to make a case without them and was faced with having to release Chris from jail. He now had a much better chance of making the charges stick. I told him April specifically told me her daddy told Christopher to hide the bullets but there was no way I would allow the children to be subjected to testifying in court. He assured me they were way too young and would never be called in to testify. He would present the evidence of their testimony in his report showing the gun was loaded in my presence and Chris had unloaded it when he knew the police were on their way instructing Christopher to hide the bullets. He told me he had a lot of paperwork to do and he would get back to me in a couple of days.

It was almost time to move. Since Meg and I worked at Zody's together it was easy to schedule myself on days and shifts she didn't work. We would be each other's babysitter saving on child care costs too. Her husband worked long days, most of the time, not making it home before she had to leave for work. Everything was finally all falling into place. It felt good and I informed my parents the children and I would be moving out. I'm sure they were as anxious for us to leave and start our new life as I was.

Things were going good. Meg and I worked well together. With Chris locked up I was able to relax a bit not having to be on guard all the time. I remembered Patti started a Friday night game night at her house after her parents left for Germany. It sounded like a nice distraction. Meg had no problem watching the children for a few hours and suggested they sleepover. Then I wouldn't have to wake them in the middle of the night to go home.

I had become friends with several of the guys Patti worked with. They were there every Friday so I got to know them on the occasions I had a chance to go. We talked about our failed marriages. Each of us discussed what we wanted in our next relationship and what we learned we wouldn't tolerate ever again. I told my friends I was planning on moving in with Meg asking if any of them could help. They all said yes and suggested we do it that weekend since none of them had any other plans. In a couple of days the children and I were all settled in our new home.

It wasn't long before I finally received a job offer from one of the banks I applied at. It was a full-time teller position at Silver State Schools Federal Credit Union to be exact with medical and dental insurance for myself and the children. I was ecstatic! I accepted the job and gave Zody's my notice. The cashiers organized a going away party for me and everyone wished me luck. Things were finally looking up.

I LOVED MY NEW JOB. EVERYONE at the credit union was very friendly and welcomed me with open arms. After a couple months I received a phone call from Patti at work. I just happened to be on my lunch break and had a little time to talk. She said she was making wedding plans. She and Tom had decided to get married before the end of the year and she wanted me to be her maid of honor. I was thrilled for them and accepted.

With all the wedding talk I couldn't help but get a little melancholy. My mind began to reminisce. It brought me back to my own wedding and how excited and hopeful Chris and I were. It didn't end up with a happy ending for us as a couple and a family but I realized I was much more self- confident and hopeful for a better life for me and my children. I was back on my feet with a full time job in banking, which I loved. It was as if my life had done a complete 360 except now I had 2 beautiful babies to give me the strength and determination to keep pushing forward.

Every morning as I got ready for work I saw our wedding rings as I reached in my jewelry box. At some point Chris had given me his ring back and I kept them together. I'm not sure why, maybe a reminder of our last happy day. I was finally at a point to do something with them so I decided to take them to the jewelers to see if I could get them melted down into one ring. I still missed my husband, the man he was when we married. I figured I would never see that man again but having our rings made into one was a way of remembering him as he was before the drugs took control.

The jeweler tossed a big, thick book on the glass case for me to look through. There were literally thousands of designs to choose from. I thought I would be there all day. After a few pages my eyes went directly to the right to check out the rings he had on display in the case. After looking at only a few I found the design I wanted. It was a zigzag, like a big Z. I called the jeweler back over and showed him the ring. He said it was one of his own designs and it would be a piece of cake. I told him I would like all the diamonds set in the diagonal line of the Z and he agreed it would look great. As I handed him the rings he said it would take about a week and wrote me up a ticket.

On the way home I began to consider visiting Chris in jail. I thought maybe I would go see him after I got my ring so I could show it to him and explain it was to remind me of our happy days. I wasn't sure how many visitors he got but I was sure he would be happy to see me. I just didn't want him reading anything into it.

The week went by fast and before I knew it I was at the jewelers trying on my new ring. It was perfect. Suddenly I couldn't wait to show it to Chris. I didn't know why I was so excited about it but I decided a visit was in order. The more I thought about it the more excited I got. I realized it was symbolic of remembering him as the man I married, not the drug addicted monster he had become and finally laying our marriage to rest. It also symbolized the end of a horrible time in my life yet the beginning of something beautifully unknown.

Ironically, I received a call from Chris' biker friend Jimmy the Greek asking if Chris could have visitors. I told him yes and I was going there for a visit after work the next day. He asked if we could meet at the bar across the street from the jail and go in together. I didn't see the harm of it so I agreed.

When I walked in the bar he was finishing the last swig of his beer. I tapped him on the shoulder and he said, "Just in time." As we were waiting for the light to change he asked me what the story was behind Chris' incarceration. He wasn't sure if the story he heard through the grapevine was the truth so I filled him in. I finished the story by telling him we were divorced and this was my goodbye visit to Chris. He told me he was sorry to hear all of it as we made our way in the front door of the jailhouse. The men went to one side to be checked in and frisked and the women to the other side of the room. It was the last time I ever saw Jimmy.

It was about an hour later when I was finally sitting in a chair in front of a glass window waiting for Chris to come in. He grinned from ear to ear when he saw me and rushed over to sit down and grab the phone receiver. I picked mine up at the same time. He said, "You look great!" I said, "Thank you." Then he added, "I just had a visit with Jimmy the Greek and he told me you came here with him. What are you doing with him?" I explained, "Jimmy called me to see if you could have visitors and I told him I was going there too. So he asked me to meet him at the bar across the street before we went in to the jailhouse. I assumed he just wanted to get the story of your incarceration straight from me because that's all we talked about during our brief walk across the street." I assured him we were not at the bar drinking together because I could tell it was his impression. Then he said he thought Jimmy wanted him to believe he was involved with me. He knew it would drive Chris crazy being locked up and not able to do anything about it. I reassured him it was the first and only time I had ever even heard from or seen Jimmy since Chris and I were together.

Feeling content with my explanation he changed the subject. "So, I hear you found the bullets. Guess I will be in here for a while." I shook my head yes and said, "I only came to say goodbye. I don't want to give you the wrong impression." He looked haggard, thin and bony. He barely resembled the man I married and it sickened me to think he did it to himself. I suddenly wanted to get out of there. I had to make it short. To my surprise he asked what I did with our wedding rings so I showed him my new Z ring and explained the meaning behind it. He put his hand flat on the window and I put mine up to his. I told him my husband Chris would always be in my heart and prayers but I had to move on. He begged me not to go as I stood up to leave. He insisted we had another 10 minutes to our visit but I told him I had said what I came to say. I wished him a good life and told him I hoped he would get clean so he could be a good father to our children then turned and left the room.

As I walked down the steps of the jailhouse I felt like a new woman. I took a deep breath of fresh air and exhaled. I suddenly had a newfound confidence in myself and the future for me and my children. I finally felt as though everything was going to be alright and the path was paved for us to move on.

A Note from the Author

Dear Reader,

First, I would like to thank you for purchasing my book. I hope you enjoyed my story but more importantly, I hope you felt it with your heart. Although it was humiliating and terrifying, my story is obviously not the worst one out there. There are women who lost their lives or became permanently disabled in similar situations. I actually consider myself one of the lucky ones. I thank God every day I lived to tell my story and I believe it is precisely why I survived.

My book started out many years ago as a simple diary, a therapeutic way for me to work through things. Over the span of 30 years as a hairdresser, I came in contact with countless people, women *and* men who confided in me. I began to see drug abuse was a growing epidemic and with it comes physical, mental and emotional abuse as well.

Every time I advised or gave guidance and/or aid to someone I relived my own pain but after a while it became a little easier as I realized this was the reason I survived my own ordeal. I was in their shoes and could sympathize with them and try to help them escape the prison of pain they were in which I was all too familiar with. My scribbled little journal transformed into a novel so I could share it with others and hopefully maybe even inspire someone in a similar situation to find the strength within them and finally take action. I know all too well how hopeless and helpless one feels in these situations and how desperately help is needed.

Back in the early 80's when my story was unfolding, crystal meth was a newcomer in our society and very little was known about it. Now, it floods our cities and poisons our loved ones who use it. The evil of it takes hold of the very soul of its user and transforms them into a devoted follower of its power. However it is important for people to know you cannot help an addict if they refuse to help themselves. I left and went back to my husband several times before I realized it for myself. I found myself at the mercy of a drug crazed evil and was almost killed as it only gets worse as the drug abuse continues. I was very young and naïve at the time not even aware of the warning signs as I'm sure is the same for many of you. Whether it's crystal meth, heroin, cocaine, alcohol, prescription pills, etc. addiction is brutal. It possesses our loved ones making them nearly unrecognizable and makes them hurt the very people they love the most just to get their next fix.

We all have a story within us to tell, some worse than others. No one makes it through life without hurdles to jump, loss of loved ones and lessons to learn from our experiences. It's time we share our stories and learn from one another rather than keep it inside because we are too embarrassed to tell anyone. It took me a long time to open up about my story because I was ashamed to admit I tolerated things I shouldn't have and made excuses to myself for a lot of things to keep our family together. I thought I was doing it for the sake of our children until I realized I wasn't doing my children any favors by keeping them in such a violent and drug filled environment, they deserved much better. Once I realized if I put the love for my children and their safety before my husband and marriage the answer was quite simple. We had to leave. I also wasn't being fair to myself. I was so broken down I started to use it myself to appease him and to lose weight and given time it may have gotten worse. I didn't want my children to have one drug addicted parent, let alone two. Staying only enables the situation to continue and get worse. It also sends an unspoken message to the abuser you accept the behavior. I know. Then when I wanted to leave I found us in a hostage situation because the abuse had manifested and taken on an evil and possessive nature. I almost lost my life so I want to save someone from going through it if I can.

I want to share my story in the hopes I will touch people who are in desperate need of a push in the right direction to end their own suffering and get on the road to a better life. Let me be your inner voice. You have to find the strength within you to regain your own power and live the life you were destined for. It's there. God gave us all the will to live. Fight for it! If I could do it, so could you. God bless us all.

www.ingramcontent.com/pod-product-compliance
Lightning Source LLC
Chambersburg PA
CBHW071310110426
42743CB00042B/1242